'When Les writes, I read. Don't be deceived by this book's diminutive size – it's like a rich, chunk of leadership fudge that you never want to end. This eye-opening, challenging, and encouraging book may be small, but it packs a big punch.'

Steve McKee, *Businessweek.com* columnist and author of *When Growth Stalls*

'If you don't think of yourself as a leader – think again. Les McKeown shows you how to be a great one. This is a must read for anyone who leads (or wants to lead) a company, team or group.'

JJ Ramberg, Host of msnbc's *Your Business*

'Les McKeown's latest book, *Do Lead*, is a thoroughly refreshing take on what real leadership is all about. It is not about heroics or headlines, it is about achieving real results in the here and now. It's short, to the point, and not to be missed.'

Rita Gunther McGrath, Professor and author of *The End of Competitive Advantage*

'*Do Lead* is a stimulating page turner that will help you grease those rusty leadership gears you've been neglecting for some time now.'

Michael Port & Associates, *Book Yourself Solid*

'If you've ever worried that your everyday acts of leadership don't quite measure up to slipping into a superhero's outfit and fighting evil, then you can relax. In this funny yet practical book, Les McKeown gets down to what it really means to lead.'

Michael Bungay Stanier, author of *Do More Great Work*

'Do you want to be a better leader? *Do Lead* paves the way to get you started right here, right now. By providing plenty of actionable insights, Les becomes your own personal mentor with the turn of every page... Do Read!'

Lon Southerland, Senior Director of Global Food and Beverage Marriott International

'*Do Lead* embraces both diversity and engagement as it speaks in understandable terms that everyone can be a leader.'

Jim McIntyre, President and CEO Otter Tail Corporation

'Whether you are a company president, a junior executive, or an intern you will gain stunning new insights on what it takes to be an impactful leader. This book is a must read for anyone looking to beat the competition and ensure you have the best people doing the best work to be the best organization.'

Justin Nelson, Co-Founder & President, National Gay & Lesbian Chamber of Commerce

'*Do Lead* is a book you wish you would have read decades ago. Brush up on your leadership skills and then pass this brilliant account on to a new graduate. The knowledge they obtain from this book will be priceless.'

Pat Smith, Chief Executive Officer of Career Systems International

'Not everyone is a leader by title, but everyone can be a leader by action. *Do Lead* will teach you that leadership can (and should) be attained by anyone, including you. Especially, you.'

Nilofer Merchant, bestselling author of *11 Rules for Creating Value In the Social Era*

'*Do Lead* is an inspiring must-read that will have you re-examining everything you thought you knew about leadership. Instead of being a trait held by an elite group of individuals, you'll find that leadership is accessible to everyone.'

Kate Marshall, Award-winning Speaker, Facilitator, Coach 'Building Business Athletes'

'In *Do Lead*, Les McKeown helps you make being a leader not just what you do, but who you are. Read this book and make a difference – regardless of your industry, background or title – every single day.'

Carol Roth, CNBC contributor, entrepreneur and bestselling author of *The Entrepreneur Equation*

'*Do Lead* breathes new life into the concept of leadership. Like many business owners, I once viewed leadership as a function of management. After reading *Do Lead*, however, I realized that every employee could be exercising leadership to achieve common goals.'

Leslie Pembrook, President and CEO of The Medical Team, Inc.

Do Lead

Share Your Vision.
Inspire Others.
Achieve the Impossible.

Les McKeown

To JMW

Published by
The Do Book Company 2014
Works in Progress Publishing Ltd
thedobook.co

Text © Les McKeown 2014
Illustrations © Millie Marotta 2014

The right of Les McKeown to be
identified as author of this work
has been asserted by him in
accordance with the Copyright,
Designs and Patents Act 1988

To find out more about our company,
books and authors, please visit
thedobook.co
or follow us on Twitter **@dobookco**

5% of our proceeds from the
sale of this book is given to
The Do Lectures to help it achieve
its aim of making positive change
thedolectures.com

Cover designed by James Victore
Book designed and set by Ratiotype

This edition printed and bound
by Livonia Print Ltd on Munken,
an FSC-certified paper

A CIP catalogue record for this book
is available from the British Library

ISBN 978-1-907974-17-5

3 5 7 9 10 8 6 4 2

Contents

Introduction

It's commonplace today to hear people talk about a leadership vacuum. And it's true – at the present time we have few real leaders we can look to, and those we do look to for leadership are judged by a low standard.

Look at any sector where we expect to see inspirational leaders – politics, business, entertainment, law enforcement – and instead we see scandal after scandal, each peeling away another layer of our implicit trust in, and respect for, our leaders.

But are there fewer real leaders? Or, as I believe, has the entire concept of leadership been distorted over the last half-century – shifting our perspective and preventing us from seeing acts of true leadership?

When we consider the idea of leadership, we see it as an elite act, set apart from everyday life and undertaken by people who are somehow special. That leadership is something 'other', something practised by people who are not you, not I.

And, of course, once we 'outsource' the idea of leadership – place it in the hands of these 'others', two things immediately begin to happen: first, we start to lose trust in the 'others'; and secondly, we get to exempt ourselves from their failures. If leadership is undertaken by people other than ourselves, then their failures are their fault and their problem – not ours. Whether it's an expenses scandal or obscenely intrusive spying or botched corporate governance or outright fraud, we get to stand aside, wash our hands of the consequences and tut.

It is said that every generation gets the leadership they deserve, and at present we're reaping the consequences of this outsourcing of leadership: our leaders are letting us down, and as a consequence our institutions are failing.

But this doesn't need to be so. Over and over again, I've proved in my own career, working with institutions, organisations and their leaders for three decades, that this slide can be halted, and real, effective leadership restored in almost any environment. It takes only one realisation: leadership isn't an elite act. We can all, any of us, lead at any time. And in fact, more of us should.

In this book, you'll learn what it truly means to lead, and how to do it (if you want to). In the first four chapters of the book we'll demolish the four myths that have paralysed leadership in our modern era: that leadership has to be 'heroic'; that to be a leader you have to be a certain type of person; that you can only lead from in front; and that leadership is only revealed at times of crisis.

Put simply, you'll learn the opposite: that leadership is often mundane; that it can be undertaken by anyone, even if they're not the recognised leader of the group; and that true leadership – leadership that really counts and makes a difference – happens every day, not just at times of crisis.

In the remaining chapters of *Do Lead*, I provide you with what you will need if you're going to step up (and if you're reading this book I'm assuming you'd like to): the mindset required; the basic skillset; techniques for dealing with the (inevitable) failures; and guidance on how to get started. You will also discover which style of leadership is the best fit for you. For most of us it's obvious when presented with the profiles I provide. You can then finesse your natural leadership style for best results.

My goal is that by the time you've finished the first chapters of this short book, you will be convinced that, rather than throwing your hands up at the paucity of true leadership in this generation, you will take a more proactive approach. My aim is that by taking away multiple misperceptions about what leadership really is, you will decide that you too can lead – and make a real difference in your sphere of influence; and the remaining chapters of the book will give you everything you need to make an impactful start.

If you're already a leader, whether on a large or small scale, I believe this book will help reignite your passion for leadership and will give you a new perspective, as well as some new tools to make your leadership even more effective.

So, shall I lead the way? Let's get started …

1

What Leadership Is, and Where It Happens

Let's start with the real secret of leadership: it happens all the time, almost anywhere you look, and it's frankly not that difficult.

Disappointed? Perhaps you were expecting something a little more ... well, challenging? That's not surprising, because for the last, oh, three millennia – in fact, since an unknown *Homo erectus* first did a Banksy on a cavern wall – we've been pretty much preoccupied as a society with the idea of heroic leadership. You know, the Neanderthal who slays the sabre-toothed tiger, Odysseus, Napoleon, the little Dutch boy with his finger in the dyke, Captain Sully (see Chapter 4), Bobby Moore – all that good stuff.

Which is fine. It makes for good reading and an endless source of uplifting quotes (great for use in motivational posters and filling all that white space left over on your team-building PowerPoint slide).

The problem is that we've become so accustomed to leadership being defined as heroic by journalists (or historians) looking for a good story, we have lost the ability to see true leadership for what it really is: an almost always un-glorious, headline-free, mundane activity that takes place every minute of every day in uncountable different (albeit prosaic) ways.

Like a sports-loving couch potato who has become so addicted to YouTube highlights, instant replays and canned post-game synopses that he can no longer bear the monotony of actually attending (let alone watching) a complete, unedited, in-the-raw football game, so we've become accustomed to the media's Hollywood-style version of leadership to such a degree that we have lost our capacity for recognising genuine leadership as it happens around us every day in real life. And when we do that, things start to change.

Compare and Contrast

Here's an example of what I mean. On the day I wrote this chapter, the first five 'leadership' stories I encountered during my usual, fairly random, media consumption were as follows:

— A profile of a 46-year-old 'whizz-kid' CEO from a hip, funky, brand-name organisation who has redefined the concept of leadership in his company based on, wait for it, his favourite sports coaching heroes.

— A politician running a not-very-tight race for office is praised for showing leadership by taking a stand on a policy that directly contradicts her party's line.

— An entire continent is castigated for a lack of leadership as the Mo Ibrahim Foundation (launched in October 2006 to support good governance and great leadership in Africa) announced that, for the fourth time in seven years, they would not be awarding their prize to any African leader.

— The CIO of a Fortune 500 company tells a leadership conference that he 'wakes up every morning filled with excitement about what [my] team of more than 1,200 employees aims to do for the day and with a drive to apply [my] knowledge to [my] best potential'.

— An academic who has taken a sabbatical to study the challenges of leadership in modern society reports that he has identified them to be 'Technology and Information', 'Resilience', 'Well-Being', 'Disruptive Innovation' and something he calls 'Environmental Scanning'.

All well and good, so far as they go – but notice how all of these stories follow the same narrative arc: the assumption that leadership must somehow be, however vaguely, connected to wisdom, or bravery, or celebrity, or scale, or great achievement – something, anything, that adds an heroic tinge. It's hard to feel that any of these well-reported stories have any real relevance to how most of us spend our time, day to day, in the real world.

Now let me share with you the first five actual acts of leadership I encountered on the same day. Notice these aren't potted stories with a moral or a point, or halo-inducing profiles, or tales of derring-do, they're just honest-to-goodness, real-world acts of leadership:

— Our team here at my business growth consultancy had to head out at 8.30am for a client meeting. My wife rose before dawn to get her gym visit in early, so our shared car would be available for my team to use on time.

— On an afternoon conference call, a colleague volunteered to drop 10 of his slides from a presentation we would be presenting the next day that was overcomplicated and running long.

— During a coaching call, a client made a commitment to me that for one week she would not interrupt others during her team's discussions and would allow her colleagues to fully finish their thoughts before expressing her own opinion.

— During a meeting at a local coffee shop, I watched as a barista stopped cleaning table tops and jumped in to assist a colleague when the line became lengthy.

— The woman who dog-sits my pooches when I'm travelling emailed to remind me she'd be picking the dogs up at 9am the next morning, and asked if I needed her to grab some dog food from the store, as she'd noticed during her last visit that it was running low.

Notice a difference between the media-reported stories and the real-world acts of leadership? Storytelling requires a narrative arc, and reporting on leadership is no different – there needs to be a hero, or a villain, or a winner, or a loser (or a video of a cute cat, at the very least). Fair enough, magazines and newspapers need to sell copies, websites need visitors, and none of them will garner much interest with stories like 'Woman Returns Car to Husband at 8.15am'.

Don't get me wrong. I have nothing against heroic leadership. In fact, because of my job (I coach senior executives) I'm in a privileged position and get to see more of it than most people. I'm a sucker for heroic acts of leadership, and watching people do incredible things under stress or navigate themselves and others through difficult situations regularly reduces me to a blubbering mess.

But that doesn't mean we should take the 'hero-as-leader' template as our only, or even our main, model of leadership. Real-world leadership is very, very different from all that the media would have us believe.

Real-world leadership is most typically understated – often to the point of going unseen by most people. Real-world leadership is most often prosaic, mundane, unspectacular.

In fact, if you glanced casually through the examples of real-world leadership I gave earlier, you probably wrinkled your brow and wondered how they could be defined as acts of leadership at all. What on earth elevates the making of coffee for a waiting line of customers to the level of leadership – isn't that just someone doing their job? Bringing a car back on time for someone else to use it? Isn't that just a common act of courtesy? And the executive who decided to try buttoning her lip and let others speak for a change – she's surely just trying to be less of a jerk, no?

What Leadership Is

Well, it depends, of course, on how we define 'leadership'. If 'heroic' leadership is a valid concept, but gives us the wrong (i.e. too narrow) perspective on what 'everyday' leadership is, what then should our definition of leadership be?

Merriam-Webster, the popular online dictionary, provides us with two possible definitions, one only a little more useful than the other:

— **The state or position of being a leader**
   (well, duh); and/or
— **The action of leading a group of people or an organisation**

A simple web search yields equally unhelpful generalisations about leaders and leadership, even from some of the more revered practitioners of the leadership arts:

- **'someone who has followers'** – Peter Drucker
  (a personal hero of mine)
- **'someone who has influence'** – John Maxwell
- **'those who empower others'** – Bill Gates
- **'the capacity to translate vision into reality'**
  – Warren Bennis

All very broad. And frankly unhelpful.

Here's my take – one which I've honed from 35 years of working with leaders (heroic and otherwise), and from engaging in occasional acts of leadership myself – which we'll use as a working definition for the rest of this book:

Leadership is helping any group of two or more people achieve their common goals.

Not very complicated, I admit, but it's a robust definition that has served me and the people and organisations I work with well over the years.

Let's break it down a little and consider the implications of defining leadership this way.

Leadership shows up in groups or teams
It's a given that leadership implies follower-ship (you aren't leading if no one follows). So leadership isn't a self-contained, individual act – it only has validity when others are involved.

Those groups or teams can be very small
At a minimum, you need only be one of a 'group' of two people to lead. Leadership, therefore, happens not just in large organisations, but also in the smallest of groups: in relationships, with friends, even (as we shall see later) in what may seem like the most informal and transient of water-cooler interactions.

Leadership can happen in an instant

While many acts of leadership are the result of considerable thought and planning, there's no knowing when an act of leadership can or will occur. If you're with one other person (or five, or 20, or 1,000) and you do or say something that helps that group move closer to a common goal, that's an act of leadership. A spur-of-the-moment decision made on the fly stands equally as an act of leadership with an agonising decision made only after sleepless nights and much soul-searching.

Leadership isn't a permanent state

In a group or team, I might do something that is an act of leadership in one moment, and you might follow it with another. Joan over there might contribute another act of leadership later on. It's important to see that even when a group or team has formally designated 'leaders' (a project management team, say, or an executive board), those 'recognised' leaders don't have a monopoly over acts of leadership. (In fact, as we'll see in a later chapter, this mindset – that only formally accepted leaders can or should lead – is highly dysfunctional and produces poor-quality teams.)

Leadership happens both formally and informally

Leadership doesn't only occur in formal situations like board meetings, on the sports field or in a war room. Groups of two or more people can coalesce in an instant around short- or medium-term objectives. Showing leadership is equally possible whether you're at a three-day strategic retreat fighting for the survival of your business, or chatting in the cafeteria with a colleague about how to ship a sample product to Beijing.

What Leadership Is Not

Finally in this first chapter, it's important for us to get out of the way some of the more dangerous myths about what's involved in being a leader.

Dangerous? I guess 'debilitating' would be a better word. Unless you're running a major military operation, no one's life is endangered when leadership is portrayed as something it isn't, but many people are dissuaded on a daily basis from engaging in acts of leadership because they've been sold a notion of what it is to be a leader that's unrealistic and intimidating.

Leadership isn't about charisma

Let's start with the most glaring of category errors in thinking about leadership – the notion that leaders are charismatic and that leadership is glamorous.

I've met (and worked for) many charismatic leaders in my time, some of whom you'd know by name and many you wouldn't. But for every charismatic leader who has crossed my path, I've met and worked with hundreds more who couldn't possibly be described that way.

Charisma, if you have it, can be a great tool for a leader to wield (it's equally dangerous if used wrongly, of course) – but it's not a prerequisite. Nor is it necessary to be a wonderful communicator, or a fantastic motivator or a savant who reads people and understands their motives. All of these qualities are helpful to have, but just as possessing any or all of these characteristics doesn't automatically make you a leader, so not having them doesn't preclude you from engaging in acts of leadership.

Leadership isn't about genius

Leaders sometimes come up with truly remarkable ideas. When they do, they get written about and lauded (sometimes, rightly so). But leadership isn't all about brilliant ideas and acts of genius. Sometimes, leadership is the opposite: eschewing the highly creative, knock-it-out-of-the-park blue-sky idea for the mundane; choosing between not very risky alternatives; or, on occasion, simply making a statement of the bleeding obvious.

At the risk of sounding like a broken record, if you have an IQ that upgrades you to platinum status at MENSA, that's fine, and you will certainly find many opportunities as a leader to exercise it – but genius isn't the price of entry to leadership. There are very many exceptionally clever people who could never, in a month of Sundays, be thought of as effective leaders – most likely your old college professors included. Similarly, I know many, many people with non-stellar IQs who are consistently superb leaders.

Leadership isn't about position

By now it should be obvious that leadership has almost nothing to do with an individual's position on an org chart. While seniority in an organisation may be a lagging indicator that someone has leadership skills, it's by no means a guarantee of it, and many people who never rise to a position of prominence in an organisation consistently act as leaders nonetheless. We'll see more about the interplay between position and leadership in Chapter 3, 'How (and When) to Lead'.

What This Means for You

Here's a summary of what we've learned in this chapter. Take a moment to read through each of the points below and make your own notes about the implication each has for your own leadership:

— The concept of leadership has been hijacked by the media and re-presented as meaning heroic leadership.
— Real day-to-day leadership may occasionally include heroic leadership, but more often than not it's relatively straightforward, even mundane.
— Leadership is defined as helping any group of two or more people achieve their common goals.
— This means anyone can engage in acts of leadership, at any time.
— Leadership happens in both formal and informal environments.
— You don't need to be the designated leader of a group to lead.
— Leadership isn't about charisma, or brilliance, or intelligence, or position – any one of these characteristics can help, of course, but they aren't prerequisites.
— You can lead. Yes, you.

Scan this QR code to be taken to a web page containing case studies and resources specific to this chapter or point your web browser to **DoLeadBook.com/ch01**

2
The Four Leadership Styles

It's the oldest question in the leadership canon: Are leaders born that way, or can they be 'made' by circumstance, environment or events? Do leaders spring from the womb fully formed with a genetic disposition to lead, or do leadership skills grow as an individual responds to external circumstances and challenges?

The answer is ... 'all of the above'. Some people are natural-born leaders; some aren't, but work hard to become so; and some people become leaders only very reluctantly. As Malvolio says in Shakespeare's *Twelfth Night*, 'Some are born great, some achieve greatness, and some have greatness thrust upon them.'

Let's look at a few examples.

Natural-born leaders

It's hard to imagine Richard Branson, Steve Jobs, Howard Schultz, P.T. Barnum or Winston Churchill doing anything except lead others. Each of them grabbed leadership positions at the outset of their adult careers (some even sooner than that – Branson, for example, was organising others while still at college) and continued to do so for as long as possible.

Self-made leaders

Abraham Lincoln was viewed as an unimpressive politician with little chance of attaining office, but over time mastered leadership as assiduously (and effectively) as he did his law studies; Henry Ford went bust five times before his motor company took off; early in his career Walt Disney was fired from a newspaper company because he 'lacked imagination and had no good ideas'; Katharine Graham became publisher of the *Washington Post* (then an undistinguished regional paper) overnight when her husband committed suicide, and, learning her new role from scratch, transformed the newspaper into a global success.

Reluctant leaders

George Washington didn't want to be the first US President, and refused to serve more than two terms; as millions of people learned from the movie *The King's Speech*, Prince Albert, Duke of York, was devastated at the realisation that he would have to accept the throne and become King George VI; Anjezë Gonxhe Bojaxhiu was 36 years old before she responded to a divine call that was to transform her into Mother Teresa; Pope Francis considered refusing the papacy, is still 'Bergoglio' to friends, and lives in the Vatican hotel rather than the grand papal apartment in the Apostolic Palace. (Note the preponderance of 'reluctant leaders' in global politics and religion – the sense of duty that causes an individual to respond to a higher call against their personal desires is apparently not so prevalent in business, sports and other leadership arenas.)

Why is this important? Because it tells us that while leadership can often appear innate – like a genetic disposition – it can just as readily be learned and developed as a skill, like riding a bike. Which means that anyone can become a leader, so long as they're prepared to put in the hard work.

Leadership Types

If this is so – that while some people are born leaders, anyone else can learn how to lead – why do so few people do so?

Well, we've seen one reason in the first chapter: media fascination with the concept of heroic leadership makes the idea of leading an intimidating one for many people.

The second reason (also based on a misunderstanding of the nature of leadership) is that many people simply don't see themselves as the 'leadership type': 'I'm not ambitious/energetic/passionate/decisive enough,' they think; or 'I'm not good with people/ideas/stress/ambiguity.'

Truth is, there is more than one leadership 'type'. In fact, there are four, and all of us – everyone (that includes you, so we're clear) – show up as at least one of these types, sometimes more.

So no matter what your personal style, no matter how you think, or cope with stress, or deal with risk, or ambiguity, or any one of a million other variables, there's room for you to lead. The only secret is to know your own style – and put yourself forward where and when and in those circumstances that your style will genuinely help two or more people achieve a common goal. Considering the four styles we each commonly exhibit when we're working in groups and teams, and learning to use whichever style is most natural to us is the key to effective leadership.

Let's first take a look at those four styles: Visionary, Operator, Processor and Synergist. See if you can tell which you are.

The Visionary

The Visionary operates at 30,000 feet, is most comfortable working on long-term, strategic issues, embraces change and risk, and needs frequent exposure to both in order to feel satisfied and useful. Visionaries are often (but not always) charismatic, are usually great communicators, and enjoy building a tight, loyal team around them.

Visionaries cycle between 'engaged' and 'disengaged' modes, alternating between bursts of creative energy and times when they shift focus in order to recharge. They usually come back from the recharge period with a multitude of ideas they've generated, all of which are prosecuted passionately – at least at first. On the downside, the Visionary's need to constantly be launching new, grand ideas and their tendency to hyperlink between multiple topics, coupled with their ability to hold seemingly contradictory viewpoints on the same subject, can exhaust and confuse those who work with them.

Using their vision, courage and ability to simplify complex ideas, Visionaries motivate others to 'ship' – get things out the door – but team members often find the Visionary's boredom with detail frustrating, as is their need to 'own' all of the team's ideas and their tendency to extremes of commitment (to a Visionary, ideas can be 'vital' and 'world-changing' one day, and wholly discarded a week or a month later).

Visionaries deliver best in those activities involving change and a minimum of routine. They need variety, accountability and frequent check-ins to make sure they stay on track and aren't distracted by their own innate curiosity and boredom.

Working for a Visionary entails long hours, mastering a broad grasp of detail and retaining a positive attitude. As a reward, Visionaries tend to over-delegate, entrusting even the most junior member of their team with tasks way above their pay-grade, and are often scrupulously loyal and generous to hard-working team members.

Visionaries tend to be found in strategic rather than tactical positions in the organisation, especially in those so-called right-brain activities such as R&D, marketing and planning. Many founder-owners are Visionaries.

Famous examples of Visionary-leaders include Thomas Edison, Steve Jobs, Sir Alan Sugar, Tony Blair and Jack Welch during the latter third of his career with General Electrics.

The Operator

Unlike the Visionary's preference for starting things – moving from one bright idea to the next – the Operator achieves endorphin release by finishing things. Give an Operator a clear task, a ball of string, some gum and two boiled eggs, and somehow they'll complete the job. Improvising and finding short-cuts, they'll get done whatever they've committed to, come what may.

Operators are happiest working at the front line translating the Visionary's strategies into action, bulldozing their way past obstacles, and are most fulfilled when overcoming problems by devising practical (and usually highly improvised) solutions. They are uncomfortable with a vacuum, preferring clear direction, and despite often being highly motivational, Operators find it hard to delegate, depending instead on their team to follow their lead and act as self-starters.

Operators are intensely task-focused and will do whatever it takes to complete the job they have in hand – even if (especially if) it means working outside the system and ignoring standardised procedures to do so. Because of this propensity to action rather than theory, Operators provide an effective reality check for groups and teams, frequently eliminating unnecessary activities and identifying redundant or overly complicated systems and processes. On the other hand, they can at times seem to everyone else in the organisation to be ruthless, roughshod mavericks, and not good team players.

Although they prefer clear delegated goals to vague or ambiguous directions, Operators work best when given broad latitude in how they do what they do. Attempting to micro-manage an Operator is ineffective and can cause intense frustration on both sides. Their impatience with delay and their maverick approach to systems and processes often make interactions with Operators defensive and issue-oriented. Conversely, providing clear direction and autonomy, being consistent in enforcing boundaries, and helping them with prioritisation and delegation can produce an exceptional Operator-leader.

Working for an Operator can sometimes be frustrating, as they're rarely around (they're usually out riding the range, getting things done) and aren't good delegators. Almost the only way to develop a trusted relationship with an Operator is to physically accompany them as they do their job – even better if you can find ways to help them be more effective by smoothing out their often acrimonious or confrontational interactions with the rest of the organisation.

Operators are usually found at leadership level in those parts of the organisation where hard work, hyper-focus and improvisation are rewarded, such as the sales, production and service functions.

Leaders with an Operator style include Sam Walton (the Wal-Mart founder), John D. Rockefeller (Standard Oil), Steve Ballmer (Microsoft) and Jack Welch during the 'Neutron Jack' period of his career with GE.

The Processor

The Processor thrives on systems and processes, delivering success and growth by iteration and constant improvement. Risk-averse and sceptical by nature, the Processor lives for data, eschews intuitive leaps of faith and bases decisions only on measurable, objective criteria. Not as naturally gregarious as the other two styles, the Processor will often build a tight team of like-minded individuals who together put in prodigious hours crunching data and running scenarios.

A Processor thinks logically, is compelled by data, not anecdote, and likes to bring order to the situations they find themselves in. They do not cope well with ambiguity or imprecision. Processor-leaders bring consistency, scalability, accuracy and an objective perspective, all of which they channel through the key metrics they use in controlling the enterprise.

Some Processors can overanalyse data to an extent that others find frustrating. Their resistance to both risk and change, their relatively steady pace of work (irrespective of the need for urgency), and the fact that they often respond to requests by saying no can make them a challenge to work with. Nonetheless, a highly effective relationship can be built with the Processor-leader by respecting their need for order, listening to them with respect and attention, challenging them constructively, giving credit where due, and refraining from hyperbole and exaggeration (which they abhor).

Setting up a Processor-leader to succeed involves setting clear, precise goals, making sure they clearly understand the organisation's overall commercial priorities (Processors can often lose sight of these in their intense focus on metrics), having patience and improvising sparingly.

Working for a Processor-leader requires an understanding of the underlying pattern or rhythm to their work (in order to work within that pattern or rhythm, which Processors often expect their team members to do) and similarly understanding their priorities (which aren't always obvious). Communicating surprises or bad news to a Processor is an art in itself, as they react badly to large deviations between planned and actual results. Most of all, working with a Processor-leader requires the ability to innovate incrementally, not in giant leaps which, if proposed, will almost certainly be rejected as having too high a risk factor.

Processors tend to assume leadership positions in so-called left-brain functions in the organisation such as administration, accounting, quality control and human resources. A great example is someone you've probably never heard of, Charles Coffin. It was Coffin who made GE into a great company, creating a machine that for years dominated global industry. Alfred P. Sloan Jr did exactly the same thing with General Motors. He took a good organisation and, by the use of systems and processes, turned it into what was, for three decades, a great company. And let's not forget Gordon Brown, ideally placed to lead the Treasury but far less suited to leading the British Government as a whole.

The Synergist

The key defining characteristic of the Synergist is that unlike the Visionary, Operator and Processor styles – which are primarily focused on the desires and preferences of the individuals themselves, in ways we examined earlier – the Synergist is primarily focused on what is best for the enterprise (the organisation, department, division, project, group, team or issue being discussed).

This detached perspective – not focusing reflexively on their own concerns – gives the Synergist a high-level perspective of the team's activities: if, as we've seen, the Visionary, Operator and Processor (or 'VOP') can be seen as the epidermis of the organisation – prick them and they'll each react reflexively, in a unique but predictable manner – the Synergist can be compared to the neocortex, collecting information and signals coming from the rest of the body, processing them, and outputting the instructions that enable the team or group to perform productively.

The Synergist's 'meta-view' is similar to what Ron Heifetz in his excellent book on leadership, *Leadership on the Line*, calls 'going to the balcony'. It's as if the Synergist views the VOP interaction from an elevated level, watching their engagements on the dance floor below, only choosing to intervene when necessary to move the process forward.

While 'natural' Synergists exist (we'll discuss them shortly), they are rare. If they were common, most teams of any size would be statistically likely to include a Synergist from the outset, thus avoiding the VOP gridlock.

The good news is that the Synergist is a style that anyone can learn to emulate, irrespective of their 'natural' style – any Visionary, Operator or Processor can (and should) learn to also be a Synergist. Although, as we'll see later, some 'natural' styles find it easier than others to do so, the most effective team is one in which all of the members, be they Visionary, Operator or Processor, have successfully learned how to be a Synergist when necessary.

Finding Your Own Fit

So, which are you? A Visionary, Operator, Processor or Synergist? It may already be blindingly obvious to you from these brief descriptions. However, if you're not sure (and remember, some people are more than one), you can find out in just a few minutes with this simple self-assessment: *http://DoLeadBook.com/quiz* (you can also find it by scanning the QR code at the end of this chapter).

Here's the skinny: It doesn't really matter which style you are. Although self-awareness is a great thing, what really matters is that anyone can be a leader, irrespective of their personal style. The 'secret', if there is one, is to match your leadership role to your style – and not to buy into the hype that being an effective leader necessarily means you have to possess the media-attractive Visionary style. Fine if you are one, equally fine if you're not. As we'll see in the rest of this book, anyone can lead, using any of the four styles – it only matters that you're committed to doing so.

What This Means for You

Here's a summary of what we've learned in this chapter. Take a moment to read through each of the points below and make your own notes about the implication each has for your own leadership:

— There isn't just one type of leader – and it certainly isn't always the dashing swashbuckler type we've been conditioned to admire.
— There are four basic leadership 'types': the Visionary, the Operator, the Processor and the Synergist.
— Visionaries most resemble the 'swashbuckling' leader: they are creative, think big and take risks.
— Operators are almost obsessed with doing: they release endorphins by getting stuff done.
— Processors are mostly concerned with systems and processes: their focus is on efficiency, consistency and scalability.
— Synergists are people-oriented: they know what they want to achieve, but they're also aware they need to work with others to achieve it.
— Most of us fit the mould of a natural Visionary, Operator or Processor.
— The Synergist leadership style is most often learned over time, rather than innate.
— You can learn to use all four styles as and when necessary, but it's likely you'll revert to your 'natural' style when under pressure.

Scan this QR code to be taken to a web page containing case studies and resources specific to this chapter or point your web browser to **DoLeadBook.com/ch02**

3
How (and When) to Lead

We've already exploded the first two myths of leadership.
First, that all leadership is heroic, and second, that you
have to be a specific 'type' of person to be a leader. In
this chapter, we'll expose and remove the third myth
of leadership: that you can only lead a group, team or
organisation from 'in front'.

The Myth of In-Front Leadership

Do me a favour: close your eyes and picture a 'leader' in
action. Take a moment and do it now, then open your eyes
and read on ...

What did you see when you envisioned a leader in the
act of leading? Chances are, you saw someone in front, or
at the head of, a group of others. Maybe it was a military

leader taking his troops into battle, or a sports coach energising her team at halftime, or a CEO on stage outlining next year's strategy to the workforce, or a hard-working teacher corralling a group of children on a field trip.

Whatever picture you conjured, it likely assumed that the leader was doing just that – leading others somewhere – physically (like the schoolteacher), emotionally (like the sports coach) or intellectually (like the CEO).

This makes sense (being a leader involves leading others – obviously), and is often true. Leading does often happen from 'in front', with an acknowledged individual paving the way with others following along. But not exclusively. Leadership can also come from within a group or team, and even, as we shall see later in this chapter, occasionally from outside the team entirely.

Leadership Isn't Always About Being in Front

There are three reasons why it's important to recognise that most leadership can come from people other than the formally acknowledged leaders of a group:

1. It frees us from the constraints of misperception

The third myth of leadership – that only formally recognised leaders can lead – is rarely stated explicitly. In fact, many organisations try to overtly rebut such a perception by espousing contrary beliefs ('We encourage everyone to speak their mind'; 'We're a flat organisation with little/no hierarchy'; 'There's no such thing as a bad idea').

But the fact is that subliminally, we all feel constrained by the cultural and political norm that defines leadership as a fixed, formal construct, rather than what it is at its best – a dynamic, ever-changing set of inter-relationships.

2. It brings vibrancy, diversity and creativity to the group or team

Sometimes – particularly in times of immediate danger or crisis – it can be highly advantageous to have 'one leader, one voice'. When the lead doctor on a team needs to make life-saving decisions quickly, or the senior pilot on a 787 needs to take action to avoid another aircraft, the clarity and lack of ambiguity that comes with assigning leadership directly to one or more clearly identified individuals can avoid dangerous procrastination and confusion.

But in most groups, teams and organisations, the majority of their interactions aren't of this nature. Whether it's building a strategic plan, launching a new product, running a kids' soccer league or managing a not-for-profit set-up to transform education, having access to leadership throughout the enterprise is a major advantage in that it brings a variety of perspectives, experience and skills to bear.

3. It produces better-quality decision-making

Finally, multifaceted leadership within a group or team simply makes for better decision-making. As anyone who has worked with others will know, there's a far better chance of success in implementing decisions when those involved with putting them into practice have a high degree of buy-in to the original decision – and what better way to achieve buy-in than to have been part of the act(s) of leadership that gave birth to the decision in the first place?

No, We're Not on a Kibbutz

Does this mean that groups, teams and organisations should give up on formal, 'in-front' leadership and simply let anyone and everyone have a stab at leading when and how they wish?

Of course not. That would be a recipe for total disaster (we'll see later how to ensure this doesn't happen).

But what it does mean is that every organisation should recognise that there is a vast trove of untapped, high-quality leadership lying dormant within their groups and teams, and, more importantly, that one of the key jobs of the formal, 'in-front' leader is to release that hidden leadership – not to keep it bottled up, unused.

How to Influence Groups and Teams When You're Not Their De Facto Leader

So, how does this work in practice? How do you – a team member with no recognition as the team's formal leader – lead from within? Try this five-step process:

1. Understand the cultural and political dynamics

First of all, it's important to understand the cultural and political dynamics that dictate the interactions within your specific group, team or organisation. Otherwise, rather than being seen as a helpful leader-contributor, you'll instead run the risk of coming across as an opinionated, narcissistic jerk.

Look for signs that 'leading from within' is genuinely encouraged and accepted, such as:

— Other people doing it and being welcomed for doing so (that's a pretty big clue right there)
— A formal leader's openly and non-defensively asking for a team member's input

— A history of bottom-up ideas being accepted and implemented

Indications that the political cultural tide is not in your favour include:

— Meetings mostly being conducted in 'broadcast mode' (the 'leader-in-front' telling everyone else what they need to know with little or no dialogue)
— Information-heavy meetings that include little time for reflection and brainstorming
— The passive aggressive pursuit of hidden agendas by individuals high on the totem pole

Just because the culture in your team, group or organisation isn't conducive to leading from within doesn't mean that you should shy away from trying it. If you have the political clout and some sweat equity to spend, go ahead and give it a shot. Just be aware that it may be hard, and that you're probably only going to see results in the medium to long term, as you first have to change the underlying culture.

2. Know your own style

Leading from within is a delicate process. It doesn't work to simply hijack the agenda and take over the discussion. Your colleagues will (obviously and rightly) reject any contribution you make that appears to be solely for the main purpose of interjecting yourself into the conversation.

Leading from within requires two things to work: first, that you have a meaningful contribution to make (more on that in a moment), and second, that your contribution is made in a natural, unforced manner that flows seamlessly with the ongoing discussion the team is having, and comes from a place of authority within you.

Where does this 'place of authority' come from? Primarily, it comes from your natural leadership style. Visionaries have their greatest impact when they're operating in their Visionary style (watch a risk-taking, swing-for-the-fences Visionary try to contribute to a grind-it-out, highly detailed Processor discussion and you'll see the very definition of someone out of their depth). The same goes for Operators, Processors and Synergists.

So, first things first – if you haven't already done so, go to *http://DoLeadBook.com/quiz* and identify your own natural style (or styles).

3. Match the issue under consideration to your style

Once you know whether or not you lead more naturally as a Visionary, Operator, Processor or Synergist, the next step is to focus specifically on those parts of the discussion to which you can speak most authoritatively. You'll probably identify these discussion areas intuitively, and will already have experienced a heightening of interest and a greater desire to contribute when they come up in discussion, but here's a quick cheat sheet to help:

— **Visionaries** have most to contribute in wide-ranging discussions about new, exciting topics. Brainstorming, problem-solving, being creative – these are all areas where other team members are not only open to Visionary contributions, they dearly need them in order to move forward.

— **Operators** are most comfortable discussing pragmatic issues around execution. Less comfortable with generating big ideas, Operators excel in identifying the simplest, most effective ways to get things done. If you're an Operator at heart, look for opportunities to help lead your team when the discussion turns to implementation and execution.

— If your natural style is that of a **Processor**, you'll find the best opportunities to help lead your team, group or organisation will arise when the most pressing need is to find ways to harmonise, standardise and/or scale the enterprise's activities. (A word to our Processor friends (of which I am one): we have a tendency to believe that systems and processes are required pretty much all the time. Which, of course, they are not – at least not to everyone else. Rein in your natural desire to pitch in continually about systems and processes and restrict your leading-from-within contributions to those circumstances in which a Processor intervention will make a substantive, strategic difference. Otherwise you run the risk of being tuned out by your colleagues.)

— **Synergists** come into their own when a pressing issue is at heart about people. Your leading-from-within will be most impactful – and welcomed – when there are personality conflicts to be overcome, when your team is experiencing communication difficulties, or some team members are feeling slighted or ignored, for example. As a Synergist you can make a considerable leadership impact any time the team is 'stuck', not because of an underlying issue itself, but because they lack the tools to manage the interpersonal relationships involved in addressing that underlying issue.

4. Watch for vacuums, blockages, and on- and off-ramps
Once you've identified your own natural leadership style, and learned to recognise when a problem or issue is ideally

matched to that style, what next? Do you just step up to the (metaphorical) microphone and take over the proceedings?

As you might imagine, the answer is, 'Almost certainly, no.' We're looking for opportunities to lead from within, not for opportunities to boorishly alienate all our colleagues by hijacking a discussion or muscling in on a project.

There may be a limited number of occasions when it does come down to you temporarily 'taking charge' (a becalmed project team turning to the Visionary to chair a brainstorming session when a highly creative breakthrough idea is desperately needed, for example; or a less-than-harmonious cross-functional group asking the obvious Synergist among them to facilitate their next session to reduce interpersonal tensions), but most often, leading from within is about making individual but tactically impactful contributions – contributions that nudge your team or group further toward its common goals.

The best places to look for opportunities to make such contributions are vacuums, blockages, and on- and off-ramps:

— **Vacuums** are just that: dead spaces that must be filled for the enterprise to advance. Maybe you've designed a whizzo new product but haven't identified the best marketing channels for it yet (cue a Visionary intervention). Your kid's soccer league has all the season's matches and dates planned out, but no one has identified the actual pitches you'll play on (time for the Operator to lead). You've just landed the company's largest account ever, but have no idea how to plan for the inventory and manpower required (Processor to the fore) ... you get the idea.

— **Blockages** occur when something is preventing us from making progress: a key contributor holding up a meeting with her hidden agenda (time for a Synergist to lead from within by having a difficult conversation); a cash crunch preventing investment in a new project (an Operator's opportunity to plough through 30 phone calls and pull in a bunch of outstanding payments); or buggy code that's delaying the launch of a new website (time for the Processor to pull an all-nighter and fix it).

— Finding **on- and off-ramps** is my favourite way to lead from within. These occur when an opportunity arises to take what you (and your team) are working on, link it to another activity, and create something more valuable in the process. The old 'greater than the sum of its parts' thing, in other words.

On- and off-ramps provide good ways to lead from within because of the added value they bring. Sure, it's great to fill vacuums and remove blockages – but in the end, you're still headed towards the same goal you began with. With on- and off-ramps, the end goal itself changes into something more valuable to the enterprise.

When a Visionary has an 'a-ha' moment and sees how the launch of new product 'A' can also be used to rejuvenate the sagging sales of complementary product 'B', that's an on-ramp. When a Processor suggests forgoing the next round of expensive and time-consuming software updates and instead taking the opportunity to outsource all of the company's IT needs, that's an off-ramp. When a Synergist suggests moving her fast-growing Tuesday morning book club out of her increasingly cramped living room to the local coffee shop, which has been struggling since the arrival of a nearby Starbucks, that's both an on- and off-ramp.

5. Contribute

So, you've assessed the political and cultural climate and established that it's OK for you to lead from within when appropriate. You've determined your natural leadership style, identified an issue that resonates with that style, and found a way to fill a vacuum, remove a blockage or create an on- or off-ramp. Now what?

How, in practical terms, do you lead from within? What does the act of 'leading-from-within' look like?

Well, obviously the mechanics of every act of leadership varies. It can be a direct action (calling those 30 slow-to-pay customers to round up their outstanding balances); time in front of a flip chart (mapping out a way to link the launch of product A to the rejuvenation of product B); a series of emails (arranging to outsource your firm's IT needs); or a hundred other specific types of intervention.

When leading from within (as opposed to leading from in front), in my experience the key factor for success is the manner in which the intervention is made. Propounding, demanding, insisting, nagging – none of this will help win over your colleagues, which, in the final analysis, is the only way you can actually lead from within.

The most effective manner in which to lead from within is to do so in the spirit of contribution. If you check the dictionary definition of the verb 'contribute', you'll see something like this: 'To give something, in order to help achieve something else'.

Think of contributing to the Salvation Army (or whatever your favourite charity is). You give something, knowing you're giving it up, to help achieve something greater. Leading from within, if you are to succeed with it, must be undertaken in the same spirit: 'Here is something I'm giving to the team to help us move forward', rather than 'Look at me, aren't I quite the leader-in-waiting'.

Let a spirit of humility and non-attachment to the outcome be the touchstone of your leading-from-within contributions.

How to Lead Even When You're Not Part of the Team

Some people (maybe you will be one of them) become master leaders-from-within. They learn, over time, to groove the rhythm of matching issues to their style, and learn to contribute back to their team in a way that others find helpful and non-aggrandising. When that happens, I've noticed a second dynamic begins to click into place: those master-leaders develop an aura (sounds very grandiose, I know, but bear with me) that permits them the ability to, from time to time and depending on the circumstances, contribute acts of leadership to other teams – teams that they're not formally connected with.

Some of this happens, of course, simply because the people in those other teams recognise competence and success when they see it, and want some of what the master-leader has got. I'm sure you've been in a group or team situation when someone has suggested 'poaching' the input of an outsider who is known for their skills and expertise in a particular area. But, taking competence as a given, the main factor that allows the master-leader to contribute useful acts of leadership across team boundaries is their non-attachment to the outcome (in turn, a consequence of their attitude of contribution).

For the 'receiving' team to be open to these cross-boundary contributions, it helps enormously that the contributor is seen to be doing so agenda-free – that their contribution is given entirely freely, without fear or favour, and without the need for recognition or praise. So, if you'd like to build a reputation for leadership that transcends team boundaries, consider these steps:

1. Work on your attitude of contribution. As I've pointed out, humility and a non-attachment to the outcome are the keys to becoming a master-leader.

2. Don't go looking for it to happen. Pushing your way into teams you're not associated with isn't a recipe for success. Wait for people to come to you for help. If that doesn't seem to be happening the way you'd like it to, review step 1.

3. Don't overstay your welcome. Don't bring your (metaphorical) hammock. Make the most effective contribution you can, check that there's nothing else pressing you can help the team with, then retire graciously.

What This Means for You

Here's a summary of what we've learned in this chapter. Take a moment to read through each of the points below and make your own notes about the implication each has for your own leadership:

— The third myth of leadership is that you have to be 'out in front' to lead.
— This myth would have us believe that leadership can only be conducted by the formal leaders of a group, team or organisation.
— In fact, anyone can lead a team – or at the very least engage in acts of leadership – without being the de facto team leader.
— It's even occasionally possible to lead a team of which you're not formally a member.
— This doesn't mean that everyone in a team should be trying to lead all the time – that would cause chaos.
— The right time to lead is when the best action for your team to take next is a match for your natural (Visionary, Operator, Processor or Synergist) style.
— Even then, there are some additional filters you can use to identify whether this is a time for you to take the lead, or not.

Scan this QR code to be taken to a web page containing case studies and resources specific to this chapter or point your web browser to **DoLeadBook.com/ch03**

4
Everyday Leadership

Time to close your eyes again. This time, I want you to picture the two or three greatest acts of leadership that have taken place in your lifetime. Take a moment, call them to mind, jot them down if that will help.

Let me share mine (there's a point here – stick with me):

— **Martin Luther King Jr's 'I have a Dream' speech:** Although I was only seven years old when MLK made this now-historic speech, it set the scene for transformative changes in the world I then occupied. It has echoed through the five decades since and will continue to do so for generations to come.

— **Steve Jobs unveiling the first iPhone:** This day – 9 January 2007 – was the first time I personally witnessed an entire industry upturned in an instant. Watching Jobs, in his trademark black jeans and turtleneck, almost playfully teasing the watching tech world, it's hard to believe that even he knew how completely this new device would revolutionise the way we all communicate.

— **Sully landing his stricken plane on the Hudson:**
When US Airways Flight 1549 was struck by a flock of
Canada geese shortly after take-off, Captain Chesley
'Sully' Sullenberger managed to land it safely in the
Hudson River off Manhattan. By pulling off this coolly
executed, daring manoeuvre, Sully ensured that the
155 passengers and crew aboard the aircraft survived.

All of these events (and many others) stand out in my mind
as exceptional acts of leadership – and of course, that's
exactly what they are. But consider this:

— Before he delivered that momentous speech in
Washington on 28 August 1963, Martin Luther King
had delivered essentially the same speech, on the
same themes, hundreds of times over almost a decade.
He had travelled thousands of miles to attend and speak
at countless rallies; he'd been sued, beaten, arrested
and jailed, and he'd sacrificed any notion of a 'normal'
family life to preach equality and freedom for all.

— Before he launched the phenomenon that the iPhone
was to become, Jobs had for years driven everyone
around him crazy with his obsessive pursuit of the
'perfect' hardware and software design for the phone.
And before that, he'd pursued a similar path (with
varying degrees of success) with other product launches
such the first Mac, Lisa, and the little-mourned Newton.

— Before he so artfully avoided disaster with a near-
perfect glide landing on water, Sully had logged 40
years and 20,000 hours of flying experience, including
numerous simulated versions of water landings, and
had researched and taught widely on airplane safety.

My point? Just this: Effective leadership isn't about focusing on the big things. It's about consistently doing the myriad small things that eventually make the big things possible.

As Captain Sullenberger himself said: 'One way of looking at this might be that for 42 years, I've been making small, regular deposits in this bank of experience, education and training. And on January 15 the balance was sufficient so that I could make a very large withdrawal.'

In this chapter, we're going to look at how to do just that – make small, regular deposits in your own 'leadership bank', so that one day, when necessary, you can make a similarly large withdrawal.

Peeling Back the Glossy Cover

As we've just seen, the glossy sheen of successful leadership is usually an overlay, keeping from view the step-by-step hard work that precedes a leadership breakthrough. This means that exceptional acts of leadership are almost always committed by people who are heavily invested (in time, emotion, intellect) in the underlying precept.

Put another way, most grand, transformational acts of leadership are built on a foundation of consistency of purpose.

Just as Martin Luther King was heavily invested in peace and freedom for all, Jobs was committed to producing the world's best communications devices and Sully devoted his career to aircraft safety, so any highly successful leader will, over time, exhibit a consistency of purpose. The greater the consistency of purpose (and the longer it is exhibited), the greater the leadership return.

Think of any truly great leader, and you'll see what I mean: Golda Meir, Cesar Chavez, Chairman Mao, Nelson Mandela, Jeff Bezos, Howard Schultz, Ginni

Rometty, Rupert Murdoch – they all share this one thing: a sometimes terrifying consistency of purpose and an overwhelming commitment to that purpose. (You'll also note that being a great leader doesn't necessarily mean using that exceptional ability for good. We could add Adolf Hitler and Pol Pot to that list and the underlying precept would still hold true. I'm going to assume, however, that you will use your leadership super-powers for good.)

What's your consistency of purpose?

So, what's your consistency of purpose? What underlying precept (or concept) so motivates you that you spend an inordinate amount of time and energy thinking about it and working on it? What, as they say back in the neighbourhood of my childhood, floats your boat?

Bear in mind that your consistency of purpose doesn't need to be directed towards world peace, freeing an entire nation from racism, founding an entirely new country, or even changing how 60 per cent of the world drinks coffee or talks to one another. It's not only perfectly acceptable, it's perfectly normal for most people's consistency of purpose to be directed towards something more, well, normal – like their family, or their business, or reducing the use of plastic shopping bags, or converting others to veganism.

The important thing is that you have consistency of purpose, not that your consistency of purpose (necessarily) be directed at something world-shattering.

What if you don't have consistency of purpose?

What if you don't have consistency of purpose right now? What if you just go about your business each day, doing the best you can, but there is no overarching cause, belief or concept directing what you're doing on a daily basis? Does that mean you can't be a leader?

Well no, of course not. There is plenty of room for what we might term situational leaders – people who simply exhibit leadership when and where necessary, do so because they're good at it (rather than feeling compelled to do so by circumstance) and are comfortable doing so in most environments. Call them 'jobbing leaders', or 'leaders for hire' if you will. And there's not a darn thing wrong with that. If you're a situational leader, and you want to get better at that, then this book will certainly help.

If, however, you want to make a difference in the world (and there's nothing wrong with that either), then it's incredibly helpful to know and understand precisely what difference you want to make. Otherwise, you run the risk of repeating the error Lily Tomlin refers to when she said, 'When I was young, I wanted to grow up to be somebody. I should have been more specific.'

If your desire is to make a transformational change in the world, but you don't feel that you've yet found the right North Star for your consistency of purpose, here are a couple of tips. **Be patient** and wait for one to come along. I didn't discover the field of endeavour (leadership and business growth) that evoked my continuity of purpose until almost my 50th birthday.

Rent one in the meantime. From about my mid-twenties through to my late-forties, I frequently identified a focus for continuity of purpose that, although I wasn't personally passionate about, I could see would give me some months or years of fulfilled toil and a sandbox within which to develop my leadership skills. Whether it was selling pizzas (when with a colleague I bought the Pizza Hut master licence for Ireland) or teaching postgraduates about the real world of business (when with a different colleague I started a business to do just that), I was able to enjoy the activity much more, and execute much more effectively, by making it, for the time being at least, the focus of my consistency of purpose.

And of course, as my own experience has shown, the best approach is to combine the two – identify a 'temporary' focus for your continuity of purpose until something eventually comes along and hits you between the eyes. If you're lucky, like me, one will grow out of the other.

A Micron Thin and a Mile Wide

Let's clear up one potential area of confusion here: being a leader who shows consistency of purpose doesn't necessarily require you to become a polymath or savant in that area.

Being committed to saving whales doesn't require you to become the world's leading expert in the phylum Chordata, class Mammalia, order Cetacea. Wanting to lead the team being sent out to open a new office in San Francisco doesn't demand that you know everything there is to know about San Francisco.

Subject matter experts are not (necessarily) leaders

In fact, in my experience, many (if not most) highly effective leaders aren't the 'smartest people in the room'. They don't necessarily know more about the matter at hand than their colleagues, and their leadership certainly doesn't depend on them having that kind of knowledge.

What's more, those people that do have that sort of in-depth topic knowledge – usually given the catch-all title of 'subject matter experts' – only rarely make good leaders, and often eschew any desire to be leaders (think of your brightest college professor as an example – probably not leadership potential, I'd hazard).

It's about adding value, not knowing more

What I've noticed in all my years of dealing with transformational leaders is that most often they achieve transformation not by knowing a lot, or by personally creating something entirely new, or by doing something heroic and grand. Although none of those are bad things in and of themselves, the heart of transformational leadership is funnelling consistency of purpose to add value to the work of others.

Take our example of Steve Jobs and the iPhone. Jobs' personal contribution to the iPhone project is well known and it's widely documented that there were some areas of the phone's design that he personally oversaw with meticulous micromanagement. Nonetheless, there is no way on earth that even someone with Steve Jobs' passion and drive could personally have developed the entire final product. Jobs' main leadership skill was to make what everyone else contributed better than even they thought possible – even if his methods were at times questionable.

Uber-leaders add value on a broad canvas

I work with many individuals who have reached a stage of development where they are widely accepted as leaders in multiple arenas: for instance, in their work, church and social life. And what I've noticed with these uber-leaders is that they have achieved that status not because they are renaissance men or women with an encyclopedic knowledge of, or interest in, multiple aspects of life; they've got there because they apply this simple principle – to add value to the work of others – in everything they do.

Watch an uber-leader at work, and you'll see someone who can't prevent themselves from helping others, encouraging teams and individuals, pushing everyone around them to greater and higher achievements.

From Leader to Uber-Leader

How does this transformation happen? How does a leader become an uber-leader?

Well, as we saw in Chapter 2, some people are born to it – it's in their DNA. But for most people, the transition from leader to uber-leader happens over time, as two specific dynamics play out:

1. Their consistency of purpose shifts up a level

For uber-leaders, the focus of their consistency of purpose becomes leadership itself. While they may start their career as leaders focused on, say, eradicating malaria, or brewing the best coffee in the world, or dominating one or other forms of media, over time, that focus shifts to the act of leadership itself.

Uber-leaders want to lead, and they develop a consistency of purpose to do just that – whatever the environment they find themselves in.

2. They put in their '10,000 hours'

Of course, for someone to simply make a decision that they want to be an uber-leader doesn't in itself make it so. To be an effective leader, there is clearly a need for basic competence in the act of leadership itself. To be an effective uber-leader requires more than basic leadership – it requires mastery.

In 1973 psychology researchers Herbert Simon and Bill Chase published a study which sought to demonstrate that no one had achieved world-class expertise in any field without 10 years of intensive practice, which they equated to roughly 10,000 hours of practice (the 10,000-hour principle would later be popularised by author Malcolm Gladwell in his 2008 bestseller *Outliers*).

Although the theory has come under critical review, I've found it to be almost universal in the area of leadership. In the next two chapters we'll be examining what it takes to lead – what the mindset of leadership is like, and what a leader's toolkit consists of. With the information provided, you can begin leading immediately. Put in your 10,000 hours to attain mastery, and you can, if you wish, become an uber-leader.

What This Means for You

Here's a summary of what we've learned in this chapter. Take a moment to read through each of the points below and make your own notes about the implication each has for your own leadership:

— Effective leadership isn't about the big things. It's about the myriad small things that make the big things possible.
— Most grand, transformational acts of leadership are built on a foundation of consistency of purpose.
— To be transformative, your consistency of purpose must be broad (all-encompassing) but, frankly, doesn't need to be that deep.
— Some people transcend 'mere' leadership to become 'uber-leaders' – people who lead in almost any arena and in any circumstance.
— They do this by focusing their consistency of purpose on leadership itself, and by attaining mastery.
— Leadership mastery may involve you investing 10,000 hours to attain it.

Scan this QR code to be taken to a web page containing case studies and resources specific to this chapter or point your web browser to **DoLeadBook.com/ch04**

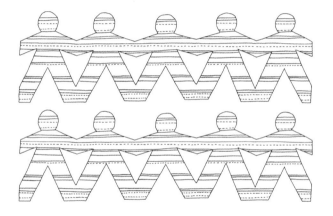

5
The Mindset

Engaging in occasional acts of leadership – if that's all you want to commit to right now – is a perfectly fine objective. God knows there's a crying need in society at large for many more people to do just that. But if you want to become a leader – someone who leads consistently and is accepted as such – then you need to hard-wire your entire mindset accordingly. In this chapter, I'll give you 20 simple words to use, which will enable you to do just that.

The 'secret' (I put the word in inverted commas because there's little truly secretive or magical about what we're about to discover) is not in becoming some sort of always-on, 24/7 leaderbot who has a compelling urge to take charge in any and every situation (I've met those people, as, I'm sure, have you, and it's not attractive), but rather in attuning your brain to shift into leadership mode at appropriate times. And what are those 'appropriate times'? Well, the definition of leadership that we established back in Chapter 1 will help us here. Remember this?

Leadership is helping any group of two or more people achieve their common goals.

So, if leadership is helping any group of two or more people achieve something, then the appropriate time to adopt a leadership mindset is when you're engaged in anything that involves two or more people.

Let me give a simple example. You're in a garden on a pleasant early autumn day, raking leaves. In scenario one, it's your garden that you're in, and you're raking the leaves both for the rhythmic, mind-calming therapeutic effect after a hard week at work, and because you know if you don't do it this weekend, it'll be a considerably larger, wetter, mulchier job a couple of weeks from now. In this scenario, you're engaged in a wholly personal activity, and one which you're free to execute as and how you like. Getting bored, or tired? Stop. Feel like raking the left side of the garden north–south, and the right side east–west? Knock yourself out. Complete the job in a manic burst or spread it languorously over a couple of days? Your call – and leadership be damned.

In scenario two, however, let's say you're raking leaves in the front garden of a soon-to-be-opened private hospice, where you've volunteered to help get the place ready for the upcoming launch day. This is very much an enterprise involving two or more people trying to achieve common goals, and one, therefore, where a leadership mindset (either leading from in front, or leading from within, depending on your role) is appropriate.

This important distinction – between activities undertaken solely on their own, and those that directly involve helping others achieve common goals – leads us to a second, equally key element of leadership, and one which is often misunderstood:

Effective leadership is goal-oriented, not people-oriented.

Let's go back to our hospice opening to see an example of what I mean. As you're still quietly raking the leaves (no doubt enjoying the rhythmic, mind-calming, therapeutic effect anyway, even though it's no longer a wholly personal endeavour), you see a swarm of other people cleaning gutters, installing a furnace, painting doors, putting up curtains. What is the goal of all this activity? If, in the course of your involvement, you choose (or are expected) to exercise leadership, to what end is that leadership directed?

Obviously, it's in order to get the hospice open on time. That's the goal. Not the happiness or collegiality or enjoyment of the people involved in the project. Now, obviously, ensuring the happiness, collegiality, etc., of the team may well be an integral element of getting the hospice open on time – a happy team is likely to achieve better results faster than an unhappy one – but equally likely there will be occasions when the equilibrium of the wider group may need to be sacrificed in order to get all of the necessary tasks completed on schedule.

All of which is to make the point that many people get this distinction entirely wrong, and start from the basis that the purpose of leadership is to build a happy, collegial team. Not so. Being good at teamwork is a highly important and useful leadership skill, as we shall see in the next chapter, but it isn't the be-all and end-all – the goal is the undertaking of the project at hand. (If you doubt this, ask any football manager who has built a very content, happy team that fails to win anything year in, year out.)

There are, of course, times when keeping a group of people happy and content is the goal itself, as you'll know if you've ever babysat five children. But those situations are rare, and are usually obvious.

The 20 Most Powerful Words in Leadership

So, to become a leader, we've identified a development need (to hard-wire a leadership mindset), learned when that mindset should be invoked (when engaged in anything that helps two or more people achieve common goals) and established that the leadership mindset must be primarily goal-oriented, not people-oriented. The question now remains – how can we invoke that mindset easily, readily and intuitively?

The answer lies in what I consider the 20 most powerful words in leadership – what I term the Enterprise Commitment. Ready? Here it is:

> *'When working in a team or group environment, I will place the interests of the enterprise ahead of my own.'*

Just advanced common sense, right? And yet, over 30 years of working with teams I've found these 20 simple words to be the most powerful tool available to anyone wanting to become a truly effective leader. Let's break it down a little:

When working in a team or group environment ...

The preamble to the Enterprise Commitment reminds us that our leadership mindset only needs to kick in when others are involved. Just bear in mind that a 'team or group environment' doesn't only involve formal, physical meetings – the Enterprise Commitment is applicable in any situation, formal or informal, where others are involved: online, offline, in a conference room, on the phone or by the water cooler.

Remember also that even a solo activity can be something that's part of a 'group or team environment' and therefore covered by the Enterprise Commitment (think back to the leaf-raking example).

We've already seen that leadership is goal-oriented, not (primarily) people-centred. And so the Enterprise Commitment reminds us to place first the interests of the underlying enterprise. I chose the word 'enterprise' carefully, in order to focus on whatever task or goal the group or team are primarily engaged in achieving.

A two-day off-site to plan the rollout of a new product? That's the enterprise, and that's what takes precedence. Chatting with colleagues to plan this year's Christmas party? Ditto. Setting up a Thursday morning book club? Same. In short, when you're leading, it's whatever you're there to achieve that takes precedence.

Precedence over what, precisely? Well, welcome to another aspect of leadership – self-sacrifice.

Assuming underlying basic competence, the single biggest barrier to effective leadership is in getting out of your own way – specifically, overcoming your own personal desires and preferences.

Don't forget, the essence, the very core of leadership lies in helping any group of two or more people achieve their common goals. Notice it's about helping the group reach their goals – not helping yourself reach your own goals. And this, in turn, means subjugating your preferences to those of the group – otherwise you're a tyrant and a dictator, not a leader (a nice, cuddly tyrant or dictator, I'm sure, but still ...).

Nor does this mean that a leader driven by the Enterprise Commitment operates at the other extreme, as a demagogue, responding passively to the desires and prejudices of the group. That's not leadership at all. True leadership involves using your faculties – your

THE MINDSET

knowledge, experience and judgement – to make decisions, sometimes hard decisions, that will get the group closer to their common goal, but doing so in a manner that isn't biased by your own presuppositions.

The question is: How can you tell the difference between when you're (rightly) using your knowledge, experience and judgement to lead effectively, and when, on the other hand, you're merely indulging your own prejudices? The answer, as it turns out, lies in something we've already uncovered.

Transcending Your Natural Style

Remember the Visionary, Operator and Processor styles? By now, you really should know which style you primarily lead with (if you still don't, go here: *http://DoLeadBook.com*/quiz). Well, turns out that most leaders' prejudices are directly linked to their underlying style. Here's what I mean:

Visionaries

Visionaries tend to prefer broad, overarching, sweeping solutions to problems – and if there's a touch of risk involved, so much the better. They're also quite capable of living for extended periods of time with ambiguity and uncertainty (in fact, they have a subtle – sometimes not so subtle – hankering for both).

All of which is fine when the Visionary is engaged in their core, 'functional' activity (assuming they've chosen a role that matches their Visionary style), but causes problems when they're leading wider teams.

Processors

Processors, on the other hand, abhor risk, don't like swinging for the fences with what they see as half-baked ideas, loathe ambiguity and uncertainty, and use safe, predictable, highly controlled systems and processes as the preferred solutions to problems. Again, just what you need from your head of finance or general legal counsel, but problematic if it's the sole or default approach taken to leading a team.

Operators

Operators differ from both the Visionary and the Processor in that they'd prefer not to be talking about any of this stuff and instead want to just get out there and make it happen. Which is a powerful attitudinal asset when held by your SVP of Sales or a head of a product installation team – but again somewhat restrictive when it comes to effectively leading a team (it's hard to lead a team if your underlying preference is not to waste time talking, let alone meeting).

What the Enterprise Commitment does, then, is to remind us that the strengths of our 'natural' style don't necessarily translate to strengths in leadership. As a Visionary, we may need to subdue our desire to always be brainstorming, and instead, when necessary, to knuckle down to the hard, brain-numbing (for the Visionary) work of grinding out the underlying detail. A Processor will need to learn that leading involves a certain amount of risk, of coping with ambiguity, and that systems and processes don't hold the answer to every problem. Operators must accept that leadership isn't all about doing, and equally (if not more so) involves passive activities like analysing, planning, assessing and even (gulp!) reporting.

In essence, to be an effective leader, it's vital to learn how to think like a Synergist – to have the needs of the group or team at heart, superseding personal preferences and prejudices.

Becoming a Synergistic Leader

How do I learn to adopt the mindset of the Synergist? If it's my natural Visionary, Operator or Processor style that produces leadership 'blind spots', how do I overcome them?

Well, the first step is to spot them. Until you clearly see the ways in which the prejudices and preferences arising from your natural style are hampering your ability to lead effectively, there's not much that can be done about it.

And of course, by definition, seeing blind spots is hard to do. So here are four tips to help you do just that:

Use the Enterprise Commitment

We've already seen the power of the Enterprise Commitment, so use it consistently. At the end of this chapter you'll see a link to download and print a credit-card-sized flashcard printed with the Enterprise Commitment for your use. Read it at the start of any group or team interactions. Print it out and keep it on your desk. Hand it out to everyone on your team. Use it.

Find a Synergist mentor

There's nothing like having a role model. If you can, find someone you know from personal experience who is a natural Synergist – someone you've personally seen lead from in front and from within with ease and grace – and ask them to mentor you in your own development as a Synergist. Of course, they won't use this terminology, but they'll understand what you're talking about as soon as you explain it to them.

Use a safe word

Give your team permission to help you see when you're making a Visionary, Operator or Processor error-by-presumption. Have them read this chapter, make up a safe word (have fun with that) and ask them to use it when they see you default to an extreme of your natural style.

Practise Using the Leadership Toolkit

In this chapter we've focused on what the mindset is for a successful leader. In the next chapter, we look in detail at what the toolkit is that an effective leader uses. The two are symbiotically connected. Not only will your use of the leadership toolkit become more effective as you master the leadership mindset, so also will your leadership mindset become more Synergist the more you use the leadership toolkit.

What This Means for You

Here's a summary of what we've learned in this chapter. Take a moment to read through each of the points below and make your own notes about the implication each has for your own leadership:

— Effective leadership is goal-oriented, not (primarily) people-oriented.
— The mindset of effective leadership begins with the Enterprise Commitment – otherwise known as 'the 20 most powerful words in leadership'. The Enterprise Commitment states: *'When working in a team or group environment, I will place the interests of the enterprise ahead of my own'.*
— Becoming an effective leader involves transcending the limitations of your natural Visionary, Operator or Processor style. Adopting the Enterprise Commitment enables you to do that.
— The Enterprise Commitment is the essence of the Synergist leadership style. Adopting it will help you develop the Synergist style alongside your natural Visionary, Operator or Processor style.
— You can accelerate the process by finding a mentor, using a safe word with your team, and using the leadership toolkit described in the next chapter.

Scan this QR code to be taken to a web page containing case studies and resources specific to this chapter or point your web browser to **DoLeadBook.com/ch05**

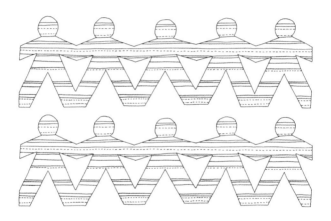

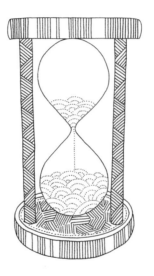

6
The Skillset

Leadership books have in general muddied the water in recent years by overcomplicating the basic skillset required to be an effective leader. The truth is that while there are some occasions when leadership calls for a specialised skill or specific experience, most leadership is at heart a relatively intuitive, straightforward act, and a basic repertoire of skills will cover 80 per cent of the circumstances in which you will find yourself leading, either from in front, or from within.

There are really only two categories of 'must-have' skills to be an effective leader: those that give you the ability to manage yourself; and those that enable you to work well with others. Let's look at each in turn.

Managing Yourself

The secret of leadership is that it starts in the most mundane of attitudinal shifts: that of taking personal control for the information flow in your own environment.

Put more simply, if you have 500 unread emails on your smartphone, are triple-booked all afternoon, and can't remember where you put the three key pieces of information you need for your next meeting, then the chances of you exhibiting any form of leadership – in any environment – are close to zero.

We need to be careful here. In recent years – the last couple of decades, really – the concept of 'time management' – or, more broadly, 'productivity management' – has achieved a cult-like status all of its own, with competing systems and philosophies, arcane vocabulary and high-priced gurus each claiming to take us to a state of productivity nirvana.

I'm not saying that every leader needs to become a productivity ninja. You may or may not get an endorphin release by achieving 'inbox zero' on a daily basis (as it so happens, I do), but it's not a fundamental necessity to good leadership. What is important is that you are reasonably good at (i.e. have a decent proficiency in, and practise consistently) three things:

Time/Productivity management

You must be able to manage your time – not just in the abstract, but in real, practical terms – hourly, daily, weekly, monthly, quarterly and over the course of a whole year. As I've already pointed out, it's hard to lead when you're perennially late, overscheduled or just plain swamped.

Despite the fact that most people who suck at this blame it on some sort of unfixable, baked-in, dispositional defect, the reality is that developing good time-management skills is probably the most straightforward, mechanical item in your leadership toolkit. It's easily taught – and easily implemented – if you simply put your mind to it.

In the section on this book's website related to this chapter we've listed a number of great resources to help you hone your time-management skills. My personal favourite is David Allen's excellent 'Getting Things Done' system, but my recommendation is to adopt whichever system most appeals to you and stick to it. Get a basic system up and running and improve it on the fly until it works well for you. Then – importantly – stop improving the system. Once you have a system that works, lock into it and move on. For goodness' sake, don't get lured into drooling over productivity porn – there's a lot of it out there, and it's counterproductive. All the time you spend tweaking and 'improving' your system is time not spent doing what it's there to help you do – lead.

Priority management
It's perfectly possible to have great productivity skills, but to be using them on the wrong things. I see people do it all the time.

To be an effective leader, it's not enough just 'doing things right' – you also need to be 'doing the right things'. Watch a truly effective leader at work, and you'll see someone with a heightened awareness of what their real priorities are. If what they are engaged in is important to their end goal, they'll exhibit apparently boundless time and energy while focused on it; present them with something that's irrelevant or a detour from their main goal, and they'll disappear before you can blink.

Like productivity management, priority management is the subject of many great books. We've identified many useful resources to help you (use the QR code at the end of this chapter to access them), but for now, let me introduce you to the single most effective tool I know to build effective priority-management skills. I call it the Single Pre-eminent Goal (SPG).

Great leaders know what their SPG is. It sits front and foremost in their minds. They focus on it when they start their day; it provides the glue that links together everything they do and say during the day; and at the end of the day, they reflect on how much closer they are to achieving it.

Of course, for some great leaders this all happens at a subliminal level. They may not use this (or any) vocabulary to describe the process, and they may not even be overtly conscious of its workings. But it still happens.

For the rest of us, it helps to make the process conscious and planned. Here's how to set your very own Single Pre-eminent Goal:

1. **You can only have one at a time.** By the nature of a Single Pre-eminent Goal, you can only have one at a time. While it will certainly change over time (usually over months or perhaps years, but not weeks), two SPGs cannot co-exist.

2. **The SPG sits below your overall mission, vision and values, but above individual strategies.** Your SPG should be the single largest transformational challenge you currently face in achieving your overall mission. Leaders I've worked with have had SPGs as varied as changing their entire product line from wood to aluminium, finding a business partner or competitor to merge with, switching funding sources from grant support to supporter donations, and designing and launching an e-commerce arm to their bricks-and-mortar retail business. All these SPGs are subservient to their respective leader's overall mission, and all dictate major strategy and tactical shifts.

3. **Your daily activities flow from it.** Unlike an overall mission, your Single Pre-eminent Goal should be specific and concrete enough to enable the prioritisation of your daily activities. Ask yourself:

'In what way is this meeting (or other activity) helping me get closer to my SPG?' If it isn't, then should you really be there? How does your SPG colour the data you read, the people you speak with, the conversations you have, the decisions you make? That's not to say there won't be other, non-SPG-related activities you'll have to engage in each day – leadership involves a fair amount of maintenance as well as forward motion. But with a Single Pre-eminent Goal now clearly defined, you'll be more acutely aware of the opportunity cost of those activities, and you may well begin to find creative ways to reduce their impact on your limited resources.

Take a little time to reflect on what your Single Pre-eminent Goal is right now, then take it out for a spin. You may be surprised at the impact it has.

Crisis management

Even a strong leader can buckle in a crisis. You've mastered your personal productivity and now focus on the right things, but then, blindsided by the unexpected, it's all too easy to get caught up in the gravitational pull of a sudden emergency and lose sight – and control – of the rest of the enterprise's needs.

Great leaders, conversely, excel in crises. They refuse to have their ongoing priorities (and those of the enterprise) distorted inappropriately by individual events.

Instead, like the ripples caused by a stone thrown into a pond, an effective leader reacts to crises with just the necessary response – no more and no less than is required to address the new situation, correct it, and return to a state of equilibrium.

Again, crisis management is a huge topic in itself, and

there are many excellent resources that can go far deeper than we can in this chapter (we've linked to many of those resources in the relevant section at *http://DoLeadBook.com*), but you'll find much of what you need to know in the next chapter – Overcoming Failure (not that every crisis ends in failure, but the principles of dealing with both are similar).

Working with Others

The second category of tools needed by an effective leader are those skills needed to work well with others. It goes without saying (but I'm going to say it anyway) that leadership involves working with other people, and the better you are at that, the better leader you'll be.

> Note that working well with others has little correlation with being liked or loved by others. I've worked with highly effective leaders who everyone adored; dreadful leaders who everyone adored; highly effective leaders who people respected at best and loathed at times, and dreadful leaders who evinced precisely the same response. Whether you're loved or merely respected is mostly down to your innate character, which I'm neither qualified nor desirous of wanting to change. Being effective as a leader is down to using the right tools, which is what we're talking about here.

As with everything in this chapter, working well with others is a massive subject in its own right, and we've provided you with links to a ton of world-class resources in the accompanying website (see the QR code at the end of this chapter), but here are the four specific skills I believe need to be in every effective leader's toolkit:

Handling difficult conversations

You can't lead if your default reaction in every difficult situation is to go missing. It is, in fact, in the midst of difficult situations that leadership is most called for.

To be an effective leader, you must be able to man (or woman) up when needed and ask hard questions, listen to tough feedback and broach sensitive topics – without being a jerk about it.

Want to know how good you are at this leadership essential? Here are five simple statements: see if they are true of you (if you find it difficult to step back and be objective about the answers, ask a colleague who knows you well to help you out).

— I don't avoid difficult, painful or negative issues and address them when they arise.
— I'm direct, but graceful and diplomatic when addressing such issues.
— I don't fudge things – I'm clear and unambiguous when discussing a difficult issue.
— When discussing difficult or negative issues with people, I work hard to ensure there are no 'hidden agendas' – on my part or theirs.
— I'm open and non-defensive when dealing with difficult or negative situations.

Conflict management

Effective leaders don't avoid conflict – nor do they needlessly create it, or make it worse. Instead, they manage conflict positively, always seeking the best for the organisation as a whole (remember the Enterprise Commitment?)

Note the interaction between 'Difficult conversations' and 'Conflict management' – and their sequencing:

it's important to build your ability to hold difficult conversations ahead of increasing your openness to conflict management. One (difficult conversations) is a key tool in managing the other (conflict management), and it's important not to plough into conflict management without first having the key tool needed to do so.

Here are some quick self-assessment questions for you. How do you rate?

— I openly address material areas of conflict as they appear in an even-handed manner.
— I encourage the airing of all sides of an issue to a reasonable degree.
— I don't show favouritism, period.
— I encourage others in conflict to resolve issues rather than ignore them.
— I act as a mediator where necessary and/or appropriate.
— I adopt a 'win-win', rather than a 'I win, you lose' approach.

Communication skills

It's an unavoidable fact: effective leadership requires good communication skills – written, verbal, listening and presentational. It's not necessary (common to popular belief) that you have to be a superstar on the stage or podium to be a great leader. You don't need to be a Steve Jobs or a Barack Obama when speaking in public, any more than you need to be Shakespeare or Tolstoy when writing emails – but it will seriously derail your ability to lead if you can't get your message across effectively.

Importantly, this means not just becoming a competent communicator yourself, but also developing good communication skills in those around you. Leadership is a little like a game of Chinese whispers, and we've all seen circumstances where trouble occurred because a perfectly good initial message was corrupted by those charged with passing it on to others – perhaps the most catastrophic example of this being the muddled orders leading to the famous Charge of the Light Brigade in the Crimean War.

Here are some quick self-assessment questions for you – how do your leadership communication skills rate?

— I communicate clearly and unambiguously, and encourage others to do so.
— I model and encourage active listening to others.
— I watch for and eliminate communication styles and methods that have a negative effect on other team members' understanding of what I want to say.
— I use plain English, and eliminate vocabulary and terminology if it is causing misperceptions or misunderstanding.
— I manage our team's communications to ensure that all team members contribute appropriately and that we don't have ineffective communicators or 'lurkers' clogging our communications.

Inclusiveness

I think we can all agree that favouritism sucks. When a team feels that a leader (whether leading from in front or from within) is playing favourites, they withdraw at best, and at worst begin to actively undermine the leader's goals.

The problem is, favouritism isn't always a conscious act on the part of the leader, and indeed, what looks like favouritism from the outside is often the leader simply trying to get the job done in the most effective way possible. (Leader: 'Jean is the best there is at this, so I always give it to her to do.' Everyone else except Jean: 'Boy, the boss sure thinks Jean is the bee's knees.')

The reality is, you can get away with playing favourites or defaulting to your A team from time to time, but for your leadership to be effective in the medium to long term – especially if you're leading from in front – you must learn how to include your entire team as much as possible.

Here are some quick self-assessment questions for you on the topic of inclusiveness – how do you think you rate? (By the way, of the four skills involved in working with others, I've found this one to be the most difficult to be truly objective about. Consider getting a trusted colleague to help you with the answers to these questions.)

— I encourage all members of the team to engage in as much of the team's interactions as is possible, manageable and appropriate.
— To the extent I can, I vary the lead role in the team's interactions from time to time to build everyone's sense of ownership.
— I watch for situations where team members have 'zoned out' in an interaction, identify why, and re-engage the team member.
— I solicit feedback from team members at the end of an interaction to gauge their sense of inclusion.

What This Means for You

Here's a summary of what we've learned in this chapter. Take a moment to read through each of the points below and make your own notes about the implication each has for your own leadership:

— There are two main skills categories involved in being an effective leader: managing yourself, and working well with others.
— Managing yourself primarily involves productivity management, priority management and crisis management.
— The concept of the Single Pre-eminent Goal is a vital tool in managing yourself effectively.
— Working well with others primarily involves mastering difficult conversations, conflict management, communications skills and inclusiveness.
— In all of these areas, it's not necessary to become a Jedi master, but basic proficiency in each is essential.
— It may be helpful to have someone else help you self-assess your proficiency in each area.

Scan this QR code to be taken to a web page containing case studies and resources specific to this chapter or point your web browser to **DoLeadBook.com/ch06**

THE SKILLSET

7
Overcoming Failure

Most leadership books assume that the outcome of every act of leadership is unalloyed success. Of course, in real life, this is rarely so.

How should a leader react to failure? When is it right to press on? How do you know when to change course? What explanations do you owe to others? How do you deal with a loss of confidence or an attack of nerves that comes with a stumble?

In this chapter we'll focus on when leadership goes wrong: the judgement failures, execution mis-steps and plain old foul-ups that every leader is prone to. We'll look at coping mechanisms, recovery routines and how to build a learning loop that ensures we don't make the same mistake twice. Above all, we'll see the positive role humility plays in truly great leadership.

Nope, It's Not the Other Side of the Coin

In leadership, failure is often linked to success as being 'the other side of the coin', as if there are two options – heads or tails, succeed or fail – and a mere coin-flip determines which you get. Failure, and its role in leadership, isn't like that.

So forget the coin analogy – when leaders fail, it isn't just that a binary outcome went one way rather than another. Leadership is a continuum, a lifelong learning process, and failure is just as much a part of that process as is success. As a leader, when a product launch goes wrong, or your volunteer-staffed hospice doesn't get its funding, or a key presentation is a dismal flop, you don't get to shrug, hope the coin falls another way the next time and move along: your future success depends on doing the opposite – analysing precisely why you just failed, and learning what you can from the experience.

Put another way, if you are committed to leadership, then knowing how to deal with failure – anticipating it, recognising it when it happens, managing it when it does, and learning from it – must become as integral a part of your practice as anticipating and enjoying success. Let's take each of those stages and look at them in more detail.

Anticipating Failure

Henry Ford went bust five times before his motor company took off. You know of Richard Branson's successes, but you won't find Virgin Cola or Virgin Vodka anywhere these days. Thomas Edison was one of the most successful people ever, in any field – and it took him over 9,000 experiments to create the first working light bulb. Winston Churchill was widely derided as a failure by British politicians from all parties, including his own, before he took over as a wartime prime minister.

We live in a society that craves instant everything – instant riches, instant mashed potato, instant transportation – and leadership isn't exempt from the notion. Fawning profiles of instant tech billionaires and tales of came-from-nowhere overnight success (especially in the highly influential entertainment industry) crowd our information streams. Couple that with the rise of the helicopter parent and the cult of the 'you-can-succeed-at-anything-you-try' child, and we have a generation of would-be leaders who often don't anticipate failure – and as a consequence are badly destabilised when it occurs.

> I'm not suggesting that as leaders we should all become moaning Minnies, dolefully anticipating impending failure with every new venture. Nor do I personally adhere to the recent glorification of failure in the 'fail fast, fail often' mentality popularised by, and widely adopted in, Silicon Valley literature. The possibility of failure is a simple fact of any activity, and should, just as simply, be realistically considered and planned for.

So here's the skinny: whatever your field of leadership endeavour, be it saving forests, raising kids, manufacturing widgets or anything in between, use this simple three-step process to build the habit of realistically planning for the possibility of failure:

1. **Run a 'red team' exercise.** As popularly utilised in the military and intelligence communities (but also used by many large corporations), the idea of a 'red team' is to put together a group whose sole purpose is to stress-test the main presumptions of a planned scenario. As you might imagine, in a test of, say, invading a foreign country, such a process can be monolithic, involving hundreds of people over weeks,

if not months. But you can run a red-team test of your next leadership assignment in half an hour with just a notepad and pen. At the start of any significant new leadership activity, get into the habit of taking a short time to play out the dark side of what could happen. (Tip: if possible, involve someone else who isn't directly involved in the upcoming activity to gain an even more objective perspective.)

2. **Set markers.** Look at your notes from the red-team activity – what signs, indications, statistics, actions might occur that will tell you if this project is going off the rails? Jot them down, as precisely as you can.

3. **Build enforced accountability.** Most leaders I see who are blindsided by failure aren't dumb. It's not that they couldn't have recognised the warning signs of a project going south if confronted with them – it's just that they didn't have a mechanism to be confronted with them. As you lead your team or group (from in front or from within) into new territory, set aside regular times to not just punch out the granular tactical steps involved in execution, but also to step back and examine the underlying data, and compare them against the markers you set in step 2.

Recognising Failure

In 2006, when Alan Mulally left high-flying Boeing to run the ailing Ford Motor Company he instituted a meeting in which managers presented progress reports on their projects using colour codes – green for good, red for trouble, orange for those requiring scrutiny. Even though Ford was bleeding cash (and losing market share) at a dangerous rate, the managers, at their first meeting, presented reports that showed almost entirely green lights. Mulally has since said that he was only able to start turning around the company once he persuaded his managers to accept that all their individual projects couldn't possibly be going that well.

We all, to a degree, harbour the ability to be in self-denial. It's easy, once committed emotionally to a leadership project, to want to interpret the data surrounding it in a positive manner. Ford Motors was fortunate that a fresh pair of eyes was able to question (and eventually tear down) the cultural environment that allowed an entire management group to wish away their problems.

Now, I recognise that most of us don't have the wherewithal to hire Alan Mulally, so here's my three-point be-your-own-Mulally plan to ensure you don't fall foul of self-denial.

1. **Don't cancel the accountability meetings.**
   Remember the accountability sessions you agreed to? I have an insider's insight for you: less than 5 per cent of the leaders I work with commit to having them in the first place (that means, by the way, that you're in the top 5 per cent of leaders – congratulations). But here's the kicker: of that 5 per cent, less than a third follow through consistently and actually have the meetings. Be truly exceptional. Don't cancel your accountability sessions.

2. **Treat data as information.** Well, duh. Data is information, isn't it? Yes, it is – but you'd be surprised (or, if you've been in leadership for any amount of time, perhaps you won't be surprised) at the degree to which leaders can allow data to become something else – an attack on them personally, an attack on their project, something the pen-pushers have to justify or

defend, an unwanted intrusion on their anecdotally based 'sense' that all is well. Data is none of this – it's just emotionless information, there to help you make better decisions. Treat it as such.

3. **Get an outside view.** When it comes to judging success or failure in real time, don't trust your own instincts. Particularly for larger, higher-risk projects, find someone whose judgement you trust – preferably someone without a vested interest in the underlying project or activity – and ask their view.

Managing Failure

You've built a process whereby you realistically assess the possibility of failure in leading. You've set clear markers that will help alert you when something is going off track. You've stayed accountable to weighing the data accordingly, and you don't blanch at objectively assessing the situation.

Now (gulp), something has indeed gone wrong. Your product launch has flopped, perhaps, or the fire inspector has just handed you a list of code violations that means the hospice won't open on time, or your team of activists hasn't received the visas they need to go on-site in Venezuela. Now what?

Times of crisis, when you face imminent, impending failure – even, sometimes, when you face certain failure – are the crucible of leadership. It's here, at these times, that your true leadership mettle will be tested. And yet, for most leaders, their response at such times is essentially improvised. Unless and until you've been through climactic situations over and over and over again, it's hard to know precisely what to do next in any given situation, and so we make it up as we go along.

It's one of the hard facts about leadership – no one ever tells you how to fail. Here's my own checklist, built, I assure you, on the solid ground of much and frequent leadership failure.

Don't procrastinate
In many leadership situations an approach of benign neglect can be quite useful. Someone pressing you for an answer to something? Let it drift and they may well sort it out for themselves. Sixty unanswered emails in your inbox? Mark them all as read and the important ones will come back round again. Let me be clear: this precept doesn't hold when potential failure looms. Once you've spotted the possibility that something might go badly wrong, block off the time you need to make a solid appraisal, and do just that.

Separate yourself from 'it'
We all have egos, and it's incredibly easy to become primarily concerned about the cost of failure to us personally, when in fact our primary concern should be first to the underlying enterprise or project. If you're trying to stop abusive logging activity in Venezuela and your team's visas haven't come through, the first consideration must be to the campaign, not to your own position or emotions. Set your own emotional reaction aside, at least initially, and focus on the thing you're trying to achieve as objectively as you can.

Apply triage principles: is this fatal or not?
If you're a field doctor faced with two injured soldiers, one of whom may recover if you attend to them quickly, and the other with no hope of recovery whatever you do, it's obvious (if heart-wrenching) which soldier you're

going to attend to immediately. And although most leadership situations are nothing like as life-or-death (or as immediate), the same principle applies: is the nature of this failure fatal or not? If your new product launch has flopped and, embarrassingly, barely no one noticed, that's one thing, but if in the process it's haemorrhaging the organisation of cash, that's another situation entirely. If the fire-code violations will delay the hospice opening by a month, that's totally different than if it means the building you acquired is entirely unfit for use.

Make the decision: fix, finish or scrap

Once you've separated yourself from the issue and swiftly diagnosed the extent of the failure, you're ready to make the key decision: what next? In my experience, there are really only three options for a failing initiative:

1. **Fix it.** When the issue is obvious and fixable, fix it. Get the money from somewhere, and bring the building up to code. Go to the consulate's office and fast-track the visas. This is usually the most obvious option, and the one we subliminally default to – how do I fix this?

2. **Finish it.** This is appropriate if the project isn't fixable but something can be salvaged and the project or initiative wound up over the medium term. Maybe the new product you launched can't be made to work in the market you're in, but can be franchised to others overseas, or you can sell the patents you developed during the R&D process to recoup some of your investment.

3. **Scrap it.** When neither above option works, then it's time to simply scrap the entire project. Because it is so

obviously a public failure, this is often the last choice a leader will make, but the reality is that it's often the best decision in the circumstances. Anyone used their Zune recently?

Learning from Failure

By far the most important aspect of leadership failure is what you can learn from the process – and if you don't turn your inevitable occasional failures into a learning process, then more fool you. Here are a few tips to help you do just that.

Have constructive postmortems

Objectively diagnose what went wrong, and resist the temptation to allocate blame. An objective assessment of the underlying facts on a failed initiative or project will highlight where responsibility lies in any case, but a witch hunt will cause people to manipulate data in self-defence, and you may never get to the bottom of what really happened. (Tip: again, as with much of the advice in this chapter, you'll get a much higher-quality degree of objectivity if your constructive postmortem includes the insight of someone you trust who has no vested interest in the underlying enterprise or project.)

Manage the cultural implications

When you examine the underlying data of a failed initiative, the goal is of course to uncover the key learning points moving forward: to approach embassies for visas (or fire officers for code clearance) earlier in future, for example, or to test your products in a more representative demographic.

But for you as a leader, there is an equally important, hidden imperative – to uncover the cultural norms (if any) that led to failure. Is there a cultural attitude of 'bring me no surprises', for example, that led to people burying adverse data? Or is there a culture of 'ready, fire; ready, fire' that pressures people to rush to action without appropriate planning? As a leader, it's your job to identify – and deal with – those cultural issues.

Learn the lessons

Remember earlier, when in the interest of speedy resolution of a failing initiative you set your ego aside? Well, now is the time to pick it up again: What, if anything, could you personally have done to achieve a better result with this project? Was there a time when you didn't listen enough to your gut, for example? Or a time when you did listen to it, when you should have been examining the data more intently? Perhaps you didn't delegate enough, or you delegated too much?

Make an inventory – it's fine if it's short, so long as it's accurate – and commit the lessons to memory.

Move on

This isn't about beating yourself up – or anyone else, for that matter. Effective leadership means keeping short accounts, both with yourself and with others.

And don't become that team for whom every discussion disintegrates into passive aggressively refighting months- or years-old history. Get your team together, agree on the key learning points, take whatever actions are necessary, and move on.

What This Means for You

Here's a summary of what we've learned in this chapter. Take a moment to read through each of the points below and make your own notes about the implication each has for your own leadership:

— No leader worth their salt has not failed at some time.
— In fact, failure – and how you dealt with it – is a better judge of leadership character than how you deal with success.
— We hear and read relatively little about how to manage failure in leadership because it's a topic few people want to talk about.
— Many leaders fail simply because they don't anticipate the possibility of failure to begin with.
— There are four key phases in dealing with leadership failure: anticipating failure; recognising it when it happens; managing it at the time; and learning from failure afterwards.

Scan this QR code to be taken to a web page containing case studies and resources specific to this chapter or point your web browser to **DoLeadBook.com/ch07**

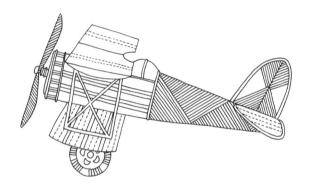

8
Lead the Way

If you've got this far, one thing is clear: you want to lead.
But how do you get started? Where's the right place to begin? When's the best time to start? Which is the most appropriate opportunity to take?

Great questions. So, rather than giving you some rote formula as a half-baked answer, let me close by telling you four short stories that may help you answer those questions (and a few others) yourself.

Start Small

In the early 1990s I was running a niche consulting company based in Northern Ireland. Started by my business partner Will and me a few years earlier, it had rapidly grown from a two-person shop to the point where we had almost 100 employees and multiple offices worldwide. The work – helping economic development agencies build indigenous businesses in their communities – was incredibly rewarding, and we were expanding rapidly.

On this particular day, Will and I were ensconced in our conference room, interviewing for a position as regional manager for a new office we were opening in San Francisco.

This was an important new hire for us, and we were keen to get it right. The successful candidate would be many time zones and thousands of miles away from us, and we would be placing a lot of trust in their ability to work without detailed oversight. Also, as it was a brand-new position, and because they wouldn't have staff to begin with, they'd have to be capable of doing just about everything well – from making high-level strategic decisions to the day-to-day grunt work of running an office.

The interviews weren't going particularly well. One candidate would knock it out of the park on the strategic stuff but would visibly squirm at the thought of taking out the trash and doing the filing. Another would clearly be a great office manager but couldn't seem to grasp what we were trying to achieve overall. Yet another seemed perfect until he confessed he didn't own a passport and had become homesick whenever he'd had to spend a week at camp.

Will and I took a break to gather our thoughts and regroup before ploughing into another round of interviews. Discouraged, we swapped views on how hard it seemed to be able to find the right person for what should have been a highly attractive position for any candidate.

As we were talking, Alycia (not her real name), our shared assistant, came into the conference room, quietly, unobtrusively, as she always did during a break. Working her way efficiently around the detritus-strewn table, she tidied everything up, putting trash in a bag and refilling our coffee in what seemed like one effortless motion. When she'd finished restoring our working environment to its pristine condition, Alycia returned – again reappearing as silently as an apparition – this time bringing with her the interview files for the next wave of candidates. As always, each file carried a cover sheet with all the pertinent data summarised in two or three paragraphs, and, as always, Alycia talked us through a one-minute overview of what she had concluded about each candidate, based on her interactions when pre-screening them before setting up the interview. Her summaries were lucid, precise and almost always right on the button.

As she left to summon the first in the next round of interviewees, I asked Alycia to hold off on showing them in for 10 minutes. I wanted to speak with Will.

Cutting a long story short, Alycia, in her early twenties and holding down her first job out of college, was offered the strategically vital, highly attractive position as our programme manager in San Francisco (and, by the way, knocked it out of the park for almost five years).

Why did we offer her the post? Because in the seemingly small things she did simply as part of her job – keeping our working environment in order and giving us pertinent, yet strategically astute information, Alycia demonstrated not just leadership, but the precise type of leadership we needed at that point in time in the growth of our business.

As I hope you've seen throughout this book, once you reframe leadership as helping two or more people achieve their common goals (as Alycia did for Will and me that day), then even simply clearing away coffee cups can lead to great things.

Start Big

At one point during 'the Troubles' in Northern Ireland there was a particularly ghoulish succession of tit-for-tat murders. One night an innocent member of one side of the sectarian divide would be randomly singled out and killed, and the next night, in retaliation, the 'other side' would even the score. One of those killed was a 20-year-old student at Queen's University in Belfast, who had the bad luck to be the last person to leave a church building late at night after a Girl Scout event. While locking up the side door of the church in the pitch-black, wet night, a terrorist stepped up behind her, placed a gun to her neck and pulled the trigger. After three weeks in a coma, her spinal cord severed, Karen died.

Just one of over 3,000 senseless killings during that awful time – but one with a twist. The girl's mother, understandably torn apart with grief, wasn't prepared to be victimised by what had happened. Seeking to understand how on earth something like this could possibly happen, she did the only thing she could think of – picked up the phone and called her local Member of Parliament. Using his connections, she opened negotiations with the paramilitary organisation that had claimed responsibility for the shooting.

Weeks later, after a blindfolded trip in the back of a black taxi, she found herself face to face with the organisation's commander (now a well-known mainstream politician). Taking out her daughter's bible – which Karen had been carrying at the moment she'd been shot – the woman started talking about her daughter, asking why anyone would want to see her dead. It was to be the first of many such visits.

Karen's mother eventually built what became a lifelong relationship with the paramilitary commander, and she was one of those who encouraged him to engage in the cross-community dialogue that eventually birthed the Good Friday Agreement, which in turn ended the most egregious of the tribal warfare that had engulfed the province. The mother, in her own right, helped co-found Prison Fellowship, a cross-community outreach organisation, and spoke at hundreds of events promoting the use of dialogue as an alternative to violence.

The girl, Karen, was my sister. Her mother, Pearl, was my mother. Pearl was, in her own telling, an unexceptional woman. A simple working-class housewife eking out a hard-scrabble living in a tough city. But she did one thing that was truly exceptional (later, I discovered it was only one of many). A time came when she could have cowered in grief, or lashed out in bitterness. Instead she chose to lead. To help an entire community achieve what had for so long seemed like a heart-achingly unattainable common goal.

I've made clear throughout this book that leadership isn't necessarily heroic. But sometimes it is. And if you're facing that call – if there's a wrong that only you can right, or a truth that only you can tell, then think of Pearl, and take the first step to make that happen.

Start Early

Like any five-year-old boy might, Thomas wanted a kid brother. It would be so cool – someone to hang around with, maybe boss about a little. But unlike most five-year-olds, Thomas was very clear about where he wanted his baby brother to come from. He wanted his parents to adopt a younger brother ... from Russia.

When Thomas first suggested the idea, his mum did what any sensible mother would do when faced with a ridiculous demand from a five-year-old. She said, 'Yes, dear, I'll think about it, and we can talk about it another time.' She assumed that that would be the end of it.

Except it wasn't. Thomas brought it up again. And again. And again. Christmases went by, birthdays went by, fads came and went, and Thomas, like any little boy, waxed hot and cold over many things. Except his little brother. The one he wanted adopted from an orphanage in Russia. That never went away. And as the months turned into years, and Thomas persisted in pressing his case, his mum and dad began to actually consider the possibility.

Initially in equal parts amused, bemused and intrigued by the possibility, the idea took root, growing over time into a mission – now for them, every bit as much as for Thomas. Web searches led to phone calls, then exploratory discussions and seemingly endless paperwork. Then, in a flurry, tickets, flights, hotels, snow, cold, buildings, people … and a baby. Then more paperwork. A seemingly endless wait. A phone call, a hurried flight, and finally, three years after first mooting the idea, Thomas watched as his mother carried Nicholas, his adopted baby brother, into their home.

The story could end there, and I could find a way to draw some sort of leadership lesson from it. But it isn't the adoption that tells the real leadership story. It's what happened next.

Having got his long-wished-for baby brother, Thomas of course experienced the same sort of post-acquisition regret that even a new puppy brings, and on more than one occasion, out of sheer frustration with Nicholas (and, perhaps, having miscalculated what the loss of status as an only child would do to his personal esteem), Thomas would plead with his mum to send him back to the orphanage.

But such moments were few and far between, and as Thomas and Nicholas grew together, Thomas decided there was some work he'd left undone. Realising that there were many more orphans just like Nicholas, unadopted, back in the orphanage, and spurred by his mother's description of the harsh conditions under which they lived, Thomas (by now having reached the grand age of nine), unprompted by his parents, launched what was to become an annual Christmas Appeal to send shoes to the children in Nicholas's former orphanage. Now in its third year, Thomas has so far succeeded in raising the money to purchase and ship over 80 pairs of slippers and shoes to Russia, as well as winter coats, summer clothes and toys.

At nine years of age, Thomas firmly believed he could make something happen in the world. By setting up a website, talking to the world through video about his passion, and making a specific and simple request of them (give me money to send shoes to orphans), he learned that he could move people into taking action. For a nine-year-old, a very big lesson indeed.

As a side note, his mother adds that he has also learned that he likes it. She said, 'He really likes leading this project. He may moan and groan when it's time to pack the boxes or when he doesn't get anything on the shopping trips, but in the end, he is really pleased that a) he is giving to these orphans and b) that he got a group of people to help make it happen.'

Most importantly, Thomas has learned not to give up. For him, sending shoes and clothes is just a stepping stone. Based on what his mother told him, Thomas's original wish was to make sure the orphanage had clean water, but the orphanage director didn't see that as a priority. So he agreed to do something the director would value (sending shoes and clothing), building the relationship, and to wait for the right time to ask once more about clean water. Every time he starts a new fundraising project, Thomas asks his mother if it's time to do 'the water thing'. And while he gets frustrated that the timing still isn't right, it doesn't stop him from doing something that truly makes a difference.

So, if after reading this book you're asking yourself, 'Am I ready to lead yet, or should I wait a while?' just think of Thomas.

Start Later

Carissa's first memory of suffering debilitating panic attacks was when she was four years old. Her home life was a mess, and though she was too young to know it at the time, things weren't going to get better any time soon.

As she grew older, and life around her became ever more dysfunctional, Carissa retreated into anxiety and depression. By the time she was in her late teens, she was, to put it mildly, a handful.

Gradually, with the help of her faith, Carissa began to turn things around. A stint in parent education while at college lit a flame in her – perhaps, at that stage, only a pilot light, but enough to start a long, slow burn.

After working as a parent educator for seven years, then as a tutor, Carissa took a position as a crisis pregnancy counsellor at a local Pregnancy Resource Centre, where she worked with (mostly young) pregnant women, many of whom had been kicked out of their parents' homes. Again and again, Carissa found herself scrambling to help her clients navigate the effects of disrupted education, minimal health care, unstable relationships, at-risk behaviours, and financial uncertainty.

In the years that followed, while Carissa brought up her own three children, the flame that she had kindled in college continued to grow and her desire to help single pregnant women only mounted, until finally – Carissa can tell you the day, it was 21 July 2010 – she knew she had to act.

Now a striking, self-assured woman of 40, Carissa has in the space of three years, with the help of over 100 volunteers, brought into being The Sparrow's Nest – a 3,700-square-foot house, on an acre of land, which is expected to house 25 to 30 mothers and their children every year, with staff that includes two house parents, two respite house parents, a case manager, family counsellor, office manager, and Carissa herself as executive director.

The woman that envisioned, raised the money for, secured and converted The Sparrow's Nest is one of the most impressive leaders I've met in my lifetime. And yet, she'll be the first to tell you that few, having met the four-year-old girl or the eighteen-year-old adolescent she was, would have accurately forecast her future.

So, if after reading this book you're thinking, 'I've left it too late to make a real difference,' think of Carissa.

Start Anytime. Start Anywhere. Start Now.

Start small. Start big. Start early. Start later.

You know what? There's only one place you can ever start leading from: where you are right now. Alycia, Pearl, Thomas and Carissa all have one thing in common: faced with the situation they were in, they each did the right thing – whatever they could do, to help others achieve their common goals.

Are you ready to do the same?

If so, I have only one request:

Lift up your head, look around, and get started.

Now.

What This Means for You

Here's a summary of what we've learned in this chapter. Take a moment to read through each of the points below and make your own notes about the implication each has for your own leadership:

— If you've got this far in the book, one thing is clear: you want to lead.
— The only question remaining is: what's the best way to get started?
— You can start small, like Alycia, who got a plum job by clearing away trash.
— You can start big, like Pearl, who helped bridge the religious divide in Northern Ireland.
— You can start early, like Thomas, who at nine years of age started raising money to send shoes to orphans in Russia.
— Or you can start later, like Carissa, who after turning her life around dedicated herself to helping single mothers keep and raise their children in a safe environment.
— Truth is, you can only start leading from one place: where you are, now. Today.

Scan this QR code to be taken to a web page containing case studies and resources specific to this chapter or point your web browser to
DoLeadBook.com/ch08

About the Author

Les McKeown is the President and CEO of Predictable Success. He has started over 40 companies in his own right, and was the founding partner of an incubation consulting company that advised on the creation and growth of hundreds more organisations worldwide.

Since relocating from his native Ireland to the US in 1998, Les advises CEOs and senior leaders of organisations on personal leadership and how to achieve scalable, sustainable growth. His clients range from large family-owned businesses to Fortune 100 companies, and include Harvard University, American Express, T-Mobile, United Technologies, Chevron and the US Army.

Based in Marblehead, Massachusetts, Les now spends his time consulting, writing, teaching and speaking. Les has appeared on CNN, ABC, the BBC, and in *Inc*, *Entrepreneur* magazine, *USA Today* and *The New York Times*.

You can connect with Les on Twitter: *@lesmckeown* or via his website: *www.predictablesuccess.com*

Acknowledgements

This book would not exist without the vision of David and Clare Hieatt, co-founders of the Do Lectures, and the unstinting hard work of Miranda West, publisher at The Do Book Company.

If you want to see everyday stories of leadership in action – the core tenet of this book – please visit *www.dolectures.com*

Index

Books in the series:

Available in print and digital formats
from bookshops, online retailers
or via our website:
thedobook.co

To hear about events and
forthcoming titles, you can find us on
Twitter @dobookco, Facebook
or subscribe to our online newsletter.